What Brown Done for Me

My 34 Years Inside the "Brown Giant"

By

Scott Lane

Table of Contents

CHAPTER 1
WOW! What a Ride!

Brown. That was the color I started with in college, and it's been my life ever since. Thirty-four years have gone by, and I've driven over one million miles, delivered thousands of packages, and spent approximately twenty-nine years on the same route. It has been a long journey, but one that I wouldn't trade for anything.

Being a brown package driver is one of the most stressful jobs in the trucking industry – and one of the most stressful, period. This profession has one of the top divorce rates in the industry, and I, unfortunately, was collectively a victim of it.

The job has a lot of structure, but there's also, at the same time, tremendous pressure to get things done quickly and efficiently. Every package has to be delivered on time, and that can be a daunting task.

So, why did I decide to become a brown driver?

After serving in the military, I was looking for a job that had a similar structure. And Brown was the perfect fit. I loved the idea of being part of a Driver Group, and the discipline and structure of the job were exactly what I was looking for.

Over the years, I've seen a lot of changes in the industry. While technology has made the job easier in some ways, it's also added new challenges.

The pressure to deliver these packages faster and more efficiently than ever before is intense. But through it all, I've never lost my passion for the job. I take pride in knowing that I'm part of a Driver Group that's delivering important packages to people all over the country. And even though the job can be stressful, I wouldn't trade it for anything. Brown has become more than just a color to me – it's a way of life now.

Every morning, our team gathers for our P.C.M. (pre-communication meeting), which is a vital part of our daily routine. During the meeting, we discuss safety concerns and any accidents that occurred in our district to ensure that everyone is aware of the potential hazards and how to avoid them. Once the meeting is over, we are free to get into our trucks and start our workday, with the knowledge that safety is our top priority.

As a heavy equipment operator, my route takes me through the rural area of northern Iredell County, North Carolina, where I pass through a charming little town called "Love Valley." The town is more than just a picturesque stop along the way; it has a rich history that is worth exploring.

Love Valley became a national name in 1970 when it hosted the "Love Valley Rock Festival," which featured famous national acts such as the Allman Brothers, Big Brother, and the Holding Company, among others. Beyond music, Love Valley is a western-themed town, complete with a horse trail, a rodeo arena, and a real saloon that serves as a gathering place for locals and tourists alike.

Interestingly, Love Valley has a dark connection to the notorious criminal Charles Manson. Manson once declared his desire to live in Love Valley if he ever got out of prison, adding an eerie footnote to the town's history. Nevertheless, for me, Love Valley is an interesting place to pass by during my workday, and I love learning more about its history and unique features.

As I drive through the area, I take in the beauty of the landscape, with its rolling hills, lush forests, and wide-open spaces. The scenery is breathtaking, and I feel grateful to have a job that takes me through such a picturesque area. However, I never lose sight of the importance of safety, and I remain vigilant in following the protocols discussed during our morning P.C.M. meeting.

My route takes me through a truly fascinating part of North Carolina, which is known as Iredell County. It is recognized as the largest dairy-producing county in the state and is counted as one of the most beautiful and productive parts of the area that can be said. The farmers you meet along the way are undoubtedly hardworking and dedicated people, committed to the land and their craft. It's admirable that they have such a strong sense of integrity, with a handshake that serves as a contract and a word that is truly their bond.

Surprisingly, our route also includes NASCAR drivers! These drivers are some of the most talented in the world, and it was a thrill to have them on board as your customers.

And then there's Tracy Barnes, an entrepreneur with a truly unique and impressive background in the hot air balloon industry. It's fascinating to learn that he was one of the pioneers in the industry and that he was recognized by Queen Elizabeth for his safety innovations. I'm sure he has a wealth of knowledge and stories to share about his experiences in the industry.

Amazingly, you get to meet them as part of your route, which overall sounds like you have a truly interesting and diverse route but also takes you through some of the most eye-conspicuous parts of North Carolina!

For decades, I was a delivery driver, delivering packages to industries, businesses, and mostly residential homes. During my time on this route, I had become so close to many of my customers that I knew the names of their children and pets and a lot about their lives in general.

Over the years, I saw two sets of twins go through elementary and high school. I had watched them grow, learn, and mature into young adults. Through my regular interactions with these families, I formed a bond of friendship with them that felt like I was part of their family.

One of the reasons I continued to bid for this route, despite the long years of service, was because of these people. They had become an integral part of my life, and I had become an integral part of theirs. I had shared in their joys and sorrows, and they had shared in mine.

But it wasn't just the job I would miss. It was the people. My close relationships with my customers have been the most fulfilling and rewarding part of my job. I had been able to make a difference in their lives, and even if it was just by being a friendly face, they could count on me to brighten their day.

As I made my final delivery, I was greeted with smiles, hugs, and even a few tears. My customers thanked me for my service, but more importantly, they thanked me for being their friend. They told me how much they appreciated my kindness and how much they would miss me.

As I drove away, I realized that the memories of these people would stay with me forever. They had become a part of my life, and I had become a part of theirs. I would miss them dearly, but I knew that the impact we had on each other's lives would never fade away. My time on this route had been more than just a job - it had been a journey filled with meaningful connections and lasting friendships.

One thing I have come to realize is that, unlike door-to-door salesmen or bill collectors, my customers are always happy to see me. I can always say I have always been treated with respect, being the "face" of Brown. I have strived to give back the same respect.

I have established a special rapport with children and elderly people. I have given my phone number out to some of my elderly customers, in case they encounter problems. This respect and concern have always served me well throughout my whole career.

As I tell my younger drivers, "If you have a problem delivery, just remember that the customer may not always be right, but they still are the customer." We sell no products, only services. Customer relations is the most important part of the job, which I had to deliver.

As a package driver for the Brown delivery service, I've often been asked why there are no older drivers like myself. After years of experience on the job, I've come to understand that it's simply a question of physical limitations.

The job can be incredibly demanding, with drivers required to jump in and out of the truck over 200 times a day. This can take a significant toll on one's body, especially over the course of many years. As a result, drivers who have been on the job for more than two decades are likely to experience problems with their knees, back, and shoulders.

At my center, I am the oldest package driver at 60 years old. In fact, we are affectionately known as the "walking wounded" at the Union Hall. Many of us have had to undergo multiple surgeries to address the physical challenges that come with this line of work. I, for one, have had surgeries to address issues with my back, shoulder, and hernia. While these surgeries have helped to mitigate my pain, they are a testament to the toll that this job can take on one's body.

Despite these challenges, many drivers remain dedicated to their work and love what they do. While the job can be physically demanding, it also helps to keep us in good shape. For those of us who have been doing it for years, it's hard to imagine doing anything else.

So, while it's true that there are no old "Brown" men, it's important to recognize that this is simply a reflection of the physical demands of the job.

CHAPTER 2
From Bicycles TO JETS

In the year 1907, there was a nineteen-year-old lad, who had a vision of starting a messenger delivery service in Seattle, Washington. He was born in 1888 in Pickhandle Gulch near Candelaria, Nevada.[1] And was the son of Irish immigrants, with a robust and resilient mother who held their family together after his father's death.

This young lad was called James E. Casey, in short, Jim Casey, and was one of America's most influenced businessmen, known for being the founder of the American Messenger Company, today called UPS.[2]

With only $100 borrowed from a friend named Claude Ryan, Jim set out to make his dream a reality,

---

[1] https://en.wikipedia.org/wiki/Candelaria,_Nevada
[2] https://en.wikipedia.org/wiki/United_Parcel_Service

which at the time was primarily delivered on foot or by bicycle, as automobiles were still a rarity.

Despite the stiff competition, the business thrived. This was mainly due to his strict policies of top-notch customer service, reliability, and low rates. Jim knew that to succeed, he had to put the needs of his customers first. So, with his partner Claude Ryan, his brother George, and a few more friends, Jim came up with a motto: "Best services at the lowest Rates."

As the years went by, the company, which was then known as Brown, continued to develop and expand. They adapted to the changing times, embracing new technologies and methods of transportation. And through it all, they never lost sight of the principles that Jim had instilled in the company.

Thus, Brown was guided by those same principles as they provided top-notch customer service, reliability, and delivery at affordable rates. And even though they've grown into a global logistics company with thousands of employees, they still strive to make every customer feel like they're their most important one.

Jim Casey may have borrowed just $100 to start his messenger service, but his vision and dedication have left a lasting inspiration for numerous. Brown became a testament to the power of hard work, determination, and a commitment to excellence.

In 1913, the American Messenger Company agreed to merge with Evert McCabe's Motorcycle Messengers. Merchants Parcel Delivery was formed and focused now on packages. That was the time the company acquired its first Model T Ford for its first delivery services. And by the year 1919, a significant milestone occurred when the company underwent a change of name, now known as UPS.

Mr. Casey, the visionary founder and originator of Brown, devoted his entire life to the growth and success of the company he created. Despite having the opportunity to pursue a personal life, he remained unmarried, choosing instead to focus solely on his passion for the business. His unwavering dedication and commitment to Brown's success became the hallmark of his legacy, inspiring generations of entrepreneurs and business leaders to follow in his footsteps.

It is truly remarkable to witness Brown's impact on transportation and delivery services. The company's arrival in North Carolina in 1967 marked the beginning of a new era, revolutionizing how packages were handled and delivered.

Ground packages were the only option available in the early days, and deliveries were recorded on a simple clipboard. Fast forward to the present day, and Brown now offers a wide range of services, including next-day air, second-day air, and international delivery options. The company has also adopted advanced electronic equipment that allows for immediate tracking of packages, providing customers with peace of mind and ensuring timely deliveries.

The evolution of Brown's services over the years is a testament to their commitment to innovation and providing top-notch customer service.

The growth of Brown over the past few decades is nothing short of remarkable. That's what always amazed me. From humble beginnings, the company has become one of the largest airlines in the world, boasting an impressive fleet of 235 jet aircraft and 293 chartered aircraft.

Each day, Brown delivers an astonishing 16 million packages and documents, a testament to the company's commitment to providing the best services to customers worldwide.

With a team of over 400,000 employees spread across the globe, Brown offers services in more than 220 countries and territories. The company's reach is unparalleled, covering every address in North America and Europe. To support this extensive network, Brown maintains a fleet of 96,173 package cars, 5,919 tractors, and over 20,000 trailers.

But it's not just the scale of Brown's operations that is impressive. The company's commitment to innovation and customer service is evident in its establishment of over 1,900 operating facilities worldwide. This infrastructure allows Brown to provide a seamless experience for customers, ensuring timely deliveries and peace of mind.

After 34 years of working at Brown, I was also a proud member of the Teamsters Union for the same amount of time. Being one of the nation's oldest labor organizers, the Teamsters had a deep history dating back to the days of horse and wagon drivers. Brown, a company that valued its relationships, invited the Teamsters into its fold when Mr. Casey began the business.

As a shop steward for eight years, I represented drivers in disciplinary hearings and learned a great deal about the Teamsters Union in the process. Over many years at Brown, I worked under various supervisors and center managers, always trying to get along and learn from them.

But my relationship with my fellow drivers was the most special to me. Some of them were as close as if they were my own brothers. We had gone through so much together, from long hauls to difficult deliveries, and we had always leaned on each other for support.

Through our union membership, we have been able to negotiate better wages and benefits, as well as improve working conditions. Our relationship with

Brown had also been positive, with the company and the union benefiting greatly from our partnership.

Looking back on my 34 years at Brown, I was grateful for the many experiences and relationships I had gained. And I knew that my loyalty to both the company and the Teamsters union would continue for many years to come.

CHAPTER 3
Your Dog and the "Brown" Truck

"My dog can hear your truck a mile away!"

I've heard that like about a thousand times. Along with "My dog only gets excited at your Brown Truck!" is another phrase I cannot disregard.

So, firstly, let me be transparent and reveal why your dog goes crazy when he notices my Brown Truck. Here's the thing.

Driving on a rural route can be a challenging task, especially when dogs are around. These dogs tend to get agitated by the color brown and the noise amplifying from the truck. Though they may hear it from a distance, it can make them bark and chase after the vehicle. As a result, drivers have to be extra cautious while driving these routes to avoid unfortunate incidents.

Instinctively, dogs also tend to sense the smell of other dogs' urine on the truck, which can further compel them to follow. These dogs are so resilient that crossing these rural routes can become a bit problematic, as many people tend to have more than one dog at times. And encountering other dogs on further routes is expected.

To be honest, some drivers are actually terrified of these dogs, and with good reason. Over the years, many drivers have been bitten numerous times, and some of the bites have been quite dreadful. I, too, have been bitten several times during my earlier days in my career. However, in the last fifteen years, thankfully, I have not been bitten. All credit to the techniques I have learned over the years and used to avoid this problem.

I have found that acknowledging the dog, speaking to the dog, and establishing eye-to-eye contact can go a long way in reducing the chances of being bitten. Carrying dog biscuits can also be a helpful way to prevent any harmful incidents. Drivers who carry dog biscuits are often those whom dog bites have victimized in the past. Overall, being aware of the risks associated with driving on a rural route with dogs around is essential. By taking appropriate precautions and using the proper techniques, drivers can minimize the likelihood of being bitten or chased by them.

Earlier in my career, the dog bites I received were "Pearl Harbor" attacks. It was one of the scariest, most gruesome experiences I had in my lifetime. These attacks were particularly sudden and unexpected. Although it's not uncommon for dogs to become aggressive in certain situations, such as when they feel threatened or cornered, it can be especially difficult to predict and prevent these attacks when they seem to come out abruptly.

So, during my early career days, once I had delivered whatever package I had according to my route, I would walk back to my truck without making eye contact with any of these dogs. I would avoid making sudden movements or loud noises and always give the dogs plenty of space to retreat if they felt uncomfortable.

However, I would still be bitten. Aggressively, a dog would pop out from nowhere and bounce toward me. It was a terrifying, upsetting encounter. Whenever I was bitten, the first question that bumped into my head would force me to wonder if they had their shots. So, I would ask their owner, "Has the dog been vaccinated?"

Knowing this information was vital because it could help determine whether or not you need to seek medical attention later. However, the owner would assure you and answer 'yes' that their dog has been vaccinated, yet sometimes they haven't. Consequently, it's not always a guarantee of the aftereffects.

Our drivers were hesitant and understood that if they reported the bite, the health department would have to come and get the dog. Occasionally, the dog may be put down if it's deemed a danger to the community. Especially if the dog has not been vaccinated, then the risk of contracting rabies is a genuine concern. Rabies is a deadly virus that affects the nervous system of animals and humans. Symptoms can take weeks or even months to appear; by the time they do, it's often too late to treat the infection.

In my experience, I have encountered situations where I have been bitten by dogs, but I have refrained from reporting such incidents to the authorities. This is because I have found myself empathizing with the dog owners and their attachment to their pets.

In some instances, these dogs have acted as protectors and guards for their owners. I have observed that these dogs are often fiercely loyal and provide a sense of security to their owners. Despite the pain and discomfort caused by these dog bites, I have been hesitant to report them and have chosen to endure the pain rather than disrupt the bond between the owners and their dogs.

Till today, I have only had one serious dog bite, which required medical assistance and taking a trip to the doctor to get a tetanus shot. Due to swelling in my leg, antibiotics were given to me for two weeks. That dog!!! I had to literally shake it off my calf. Even though it was a small dog that appeared totally harmless, its teeth were just as sharp as razors. Small dogs tend to bite more than the big ones. This was one of them. Unfortunately, they had to come and get the dog – only to find out that it did not have its shots! I was puzzled.

It was a "Peal Harbor" job, as well.

Another close call was when a woman and child came to receive the package. As they were coming, a German shepherd was tracking me from a distance. I set the package down to record the delivery when it lunged at my throat. It was bristly and tough. I hit him with my electronic board to knock him away. If I weren't fast enough, for sure, my throat would split out.

I apologized to the woman for my "French" words. Honestly, I was outraged and upset. Of course, she apologized to me as well. She had forgotten to put the dog up when I'd arrived. So, I have seen some really horrific dog bites. One driver had to have stitches inside other stitches due to a vicious bite by a German shepherd. He now always carries dog biscuits!

Another horrific bite came when the driver hit a dog and was helping the owner put the dog into a truck to take it to the Vet. When the dog lashed onto his hand and bit him, this required several stitches to his hand.

One of the most depressing parts of this job is running over someone's house dog. Accidentally harming an animal is one of the most distressing occurrences, mainly when the animal is someone's beloved. It can and does ruin your whole day! Taking risks because of these dogs while on the road is dangerous for both yourself and others. I have almost wrecked my truck on occasion to avoid hitting these dogs. Once, I nearly turned my truck over, intending to avoid hitting the dog.

One of these days, there was a dog who always loved to run at my truck. I was going through the neighborhood, and this actually startled the dog. He was a rescue, a mixed-breed dog that a family owned.

All of a sudden, the dog lunged at my truck. I slammed on my brakes but could not avoid hitting him. I immediately stopped my vehicle and went to tell the family. I will never forget the screams and wailing from the whole family that day. It was a traumatic situation. Seeing the kids crying and weeping over their dog was terribly painful and devastating. Although it wasn't my intention, I will never forget it.

My job was to bring happiness and good deliverables to people, and in this case, I had brought sorrow, even though I couldn't help it. When these types of situations occur, I am required to report them to my supervisor. If a dog is hit in a private driveway, a driver could potentially be changed (by Brown) with evidence and an accident. No charges are possible if a dog is on a public road.

In Iredell County, it is mandatory to keep dogs on a leash, which is enforced to prevent any unfortunate incidents that may cause liability issues for our drivers. During our P.C.M. (Pre-Communication Meeting) sessions, dog bites are a common topic of discussion among our drivers. They often share their experiences and stories about encountering dogs while on their routes.

However, one of the most significant problems that our drivers face is when more than one dog is present, which can lead to accidents. For instance, a group of dogs can get too close to the truck, and one dog may push another dog under the wheels. Therefore, it is crucial to exercise extra caution when such situations arise to avoid any unfortunate incidents.

The most traumatic accident with a dog, which still haunts me today, was when I killed the dog of a little girl on my route. The dog loved to chase my truck. When I stopped and told the mother, seeing the little girl cry, it really upset me. I remember this incident today. The little girl is now a teenager. Thankfully, she hasn't held it against me, but every time I stop at that house, I still remember that tragic day—just like it happened yesterday.

CHAPTER 4
Danger Lurking

In the job of delivering packages and parcels, particularly for a company like Brown (UPS), there are several potential dangers or hazards that workers may encounter. These include traffic accidents, physical strain, weather conditions, dog attacks, workplace violence, ergonomic issues, fatigue, stress, slips, trips, and falls. To mitigate these dangers, it's essential to prioritize safety through comprehensive training programs and safety equipment.

Brown (UPS) drivers spend a significant amount of time on the road, driving delivery trucks to various locations. The risk of traffic accidents, including collisions with other vehicles or pedestrians, is a constant concern.

Throughout my driving career, I have experienced several close calls while on the road, where I narrowly avoided collisions with other vehicles. Fortunately, my extensive safety training and experience have served me well, enabling me to stay alive and safe on the roads. Despite the inherent risks of the job, I have driven over a million miles in my trusty Brown truck, most of which has been on rural roads.

Rural roads are notorious for being more dangerous than urban roads, with higher speed limits and less traffic enforcement, making fatal accidents more likely to occur. As a result, I have had to be extra vigilant while driving, constantly looking out for potential hazards and taking appropriate action to avoid them.

However, even with my best efforts, my truck's mirrors have been hit twice by other trucks. The sound of this occurrence is deafening, similar to the discharge of a shotgun near my head. The impact caused the glass to shatter, resulting in cuts on my head, neck, and shoulders. It was like an explosion of glass, which was incredibly dangerous.

Luckily, I was wearing glasses both times, which kept my eyes safe from the flying glass shards.

Over the course of my career, on several occasions, cars have pulled out in front of me unexpectedly, endangering my safety and that of other motorists. Thankfully, my quick reflexes and the timely use of my horn have saved me from many accidents. Even when I had to use the horn, I always made sure to wave courteously to the other driver to acknowledge the situation and avoid any unnecessary confrontation.

I have also had several encounters with vehicles that cross the center line as I approach them. This was an extremely dangerous situation, as there was a high risk of head-on collisions. However, once again, my horn saved me from the worst. By alerting the other driver, I was able to avoid potentially life-threatening crashes.

Apart from vehicular accidents, I have also faced other types of hazards on the road. One particularly memorable incident occurred one night when I was traveling down a two-lane road at approximately 60 mph. Suddenly, I saw a large black cow right in the middle of the road. With very little time to react, I had to slam on the brakes and swerve sharply to avoid hitting the animal. Thanks to my quick thinking and reflexes, I was able to slow down and narrowly miss the cow, thereby avoiding a catastrophic collision.

Also, one fateful night, I was driving down a long, deserted rural road with nothing but the sound of the wind rushing past my car. I was cruising at a speed of around 60 miles per hour, feeling the thrill of the open road.

Suddenly, out of the corner of my eye, I caught a glimpse of movement. I turned my head to look and saw a doe running frantically in my direction. It was rutting season, and it seemed like a buck was chasing her. Without warning, the doe leaped onto the road just as I was about to pass by. I tried to swerve, but it was too late. The doe slammed into the front bumper of my car with a sickening thud.

I was driving a Brown delivery truck, which had a front bumper made of ¼ inch steel, the most vital part of the entire truck. But even that couldn't withstand the force of the impact. The bumper bent inwards with a deafeningly loud bang, like a clap of thunder on a stormy night. For a moment, it felt like the whole world had come to a halt.

Delivering packages and parcels often involves lifting, carrying, and maneuvering heavy objects. This repetitive strain can lead to injuries such as strains, sprains, and musculoskeletal disorders.

The closest I have ever come to being seriously injured was when I was going into a driveway to deliver a package. I was driving into a driveway to drop off a package when, out of nowhere, a large limb suddenly collided with the top of my truck. Before I knew it, the limb had shot through the driver's side front glass, shattering it into a million pieces.

It was only by sheer luck that I escaped serious injury. The limb had missed my head by mere inches, and I could feel the wind caused by its passage over my shoulder. Glass flew everywhere. Until that moment, the limb had always cleared my truck, but that day was different.

I couldn't help but feel that something or someone was watching over me that day. The incident left me feeling grateful to still be alive and not in the hospital or worse.

Exposure to various weather conditions is another tough hassle for our drivers, including extreme heat, cold, rain, snow, and ice. These conditions can create hazardous driving conditions and increase the risk of slips, trips, and falls.

During the early stages of my career, I encountered a life-altering accident due to the weather. It was a rainy day, and the roads were slick, making it difficult to maneuver the vehicle. As I approached a curve, my truck began to spin out of control. Before I knew it, it had turned over and landed against a telephone pole.

Fortunately, I had my seat belt on at the time, which kept me hanging in my seat sideways. After struggling to free myself from the seat belt, I managed to get out of the truck. As fate would have it, a state trooper was the first person to arrive at the scene of the accident. Although I've been a good ole' hardcore Brown driver in the most challenging moments, I still received two tickets in the process. One was for going "too fast for conditions," and the other was for "improper equipment" because my truck's tires were slick.

I was fully aware that the responsibility for the accident was mine since I was supposed to check the vehicle before using it, but it was not my regular truck. Just a few days before the incident, I had lost my father, and this was my first day back at work after burying him. I was still in mourning.

Driving in inclement weather has been one of the major challenges I have faced repetitively. Ice and snow on rutted roads are very dangerous. I always try to make good driving decisions, but in spite of that, I have not always been able to avoid getting stuck or sliding off the road. I have been very fortunate to be on a rural route where tractors and 4-wheel-drive vehicles have come to my rescue.

As I previously mentioned, dogs are a common hazard faced by mail carriers and delivery workers. However, other animals also pose significant risks. One incident I can never forget happened on a regular day when I was assigned to deliver a package to a customer.

As I approached the door, I suddenly found myself surrounded by a swarm of black jacket bees. I had no idea where they came from. In no time, they started attacking me aggressively, stinging me repeatedly all over my body. I was stung around twenty times. In a panic, I started swatting the bees with the package, hoping to get away from them. However, my attempts were in vain, and I ended up destroying the package in the process. Luckily, the contents of the package were not damaged by the attack, but I was severely stung on my neck and face.

Then, there was the day I got stung by a Japanese hornet. Almost immediately, my arm began to swell, and I could feel my throat starting to close up. I knew I had to act quickly and headed to urgent care for medical attention.

Yet, that wasn't the only episode. Very soon after that, nature's creatures again crossed my path. While sitting in my truck, I suddenly felt a sharp pain on my forehead. Upon closer inspection, I realized that I had been bitten by a brown recluse spider. I was immediately rushed to the emergency room for treatment. It took five long months for the bite to completely heal, leaving behind two deep holes in my forehead as a reminder of the ordeal.

Despite these experiences, I remain in awe of the power and beauty of nature. Though it's been one hell of a ride, I've had my moments. I now take extra precautions to protect myself from its dangers, and luckily, I have been saved from a number of other mishaps.

In December 2013, I was fortunate enough to be inducted into the prestigious Circle of Honor for Brown, an award that recognizes 25 years of safe driving. This honor is only bestowed upon select Brown drivers who have displayed an exceptional commitment to safe driving practices over the course of their careers.

As a recipient of this award, I was asked to address the whole driver group and share my thoughts on this achievement. During my speech, I took the opportunity to reflect on a fateful day 25 years ago that changed my perspective on driving safety. I shared my personal experience with the drivers and how it helped me learn from my mistakes. I hoped that my story would resonate with them and inspire them to avoid making the same mistake I did all those years ago.

As a driver, I understand the importance of safe driving practices and the impact they have on the lives of others. Being recognized by Brown and being inducted into the Circle of Honor is a true testament to my commitment to safe driving, and I am proud to be a part of this elite group of drivers who share the same values as I do.

CHAPTER 5
You Never Know What You Will See

Every day, as we embark on our daily route, we are often faced with unpredictable situations that keep us on edge. These elements of uncertainty present a new challenge, a new opportunity, or a new experience we must navigate.

You never know what to expect as surprises lurk around every corner. The unexpected twists and turns whenever you encounter new people, unexpected challenges, overcome obstacles, discover new things, or stumble upon exciting opportunities are always something to look forward to. This unpredictability is what keeps us engaged and alive.

It is what makes life an adventure, keeping us on our toes. These unexpected moments in store for us change not only our perspectives but also grant us the privilege to do something phenomenal. I, too, have been in such positions and situations a couple of times.

During my regular delivery route, I came across a farm located along my route. As I drew closer to the farm, I noticed an elderly gentleman lying unconscious on the ground beside his tractor. Upon closer inspection, I realized that he was the 80-year-old owner of the farm.

He had sustained a severe injury to his head, which had swelled to the size of an egg due to the impact of his fall against the side of the tractor. The sight of the poor man lying helpless on the ground was truly alarming and immediately required attention. I could see that he was in a critical state and required urgent medical attention.

This incident occurred during a time when mobile communications were not as prevalent as they are today, and I found myself facing a difficult situation without the ability to contact my center for assistance. It was a challenging dilemma that required me to rely solely on my own resources to resolve.

When I found him, he was barely coherent, and I almost stumbled upon him, my heart sinking. It was a dreadful feeling that something was terribly wrong. His body was limp, his speech was slurred, and his movements were barely perceptible.

I realized that he urgently needed medical attention, and every passing moment was crucial for his survival. I sprang into action and raced towards his house, frantically searching for a phone that could connect me with emergency medical services. However, the house was eerily quiet, and my eyes darted around, desperately seeking any means of communication.

With my heart pounding in my chest, I knew that time was running out, and every second counted in this race against the clock.

So, I frantically searched, with my mind active all over the place, with worry. Finally, there it was, hidden behind his "easy" chair. Without a second thought, I immediately called my center and asked them to contact 911, giving them directions to our location. I stayed with him, talking to him and reassuring him until the ambulance arrived. It was a nerve-wracking experience, but I knew I had to stay calm and collect to help him through it. But it was a moment. Sadly, it was the last day that he lived in his house for 80 years.

Afterward, his family wrote me a heartfelt thank-you note expressing their gratitude for my assistance during their loved one's emergency. It was a kind gesture that touched me deeply. I still see his grandsons on a daily basis, and they often thank me for helping their grandfather. I always humbly respond by telling them that anyone in my position would have done the same thing. It's just human nature to help others in need.

As I was driving along my usual delivery route, another time, I suddenly heard a woman's frantic cries for help. I immediately parked my truck and ran to see what was happening. As I approached the woman's house, I could see that she was in distress and that her house was on fire.

I knew that I had to act quickly to ensure her safety and prevent any further damage. Without hesitation, I sprinted into the house to assess the situation. The flames were already rising from the top of her mantle, and I could feel the heat emanating from them. I quickly went to the kitchen sink and filled a bucket with water. Using the bucket, I doused the flames until they were completely extinguished.

After ensuring that the fire was under control, I made my way out of the house and back to my truck. As I was driving away, I saw a convoy of fire trucks approaching the area. It was reassuring to know that the safety measures in the neighborhood were efficient and reliable.

This experience has taught me the importance of being alert and prepared for any situation that may arise while on the job. It also reminded me of the value of quick action, as my swift response helped prevent further damage to the woman's home and ensured her safety.

One snowy day, as I was driving down a deserted road, I noticed a young boy stuck on the side of the road. He was frantically trying to free himself, but his pants had become entangled with the bicycle's sprockets. I could see he was shivering in the cold, and it was evident he needed immediate help.

So, without any second thought, I pulled over my car and rushed to his aid. The boy was caught in such a way that he couldn't move or do anything about it. I quickly took out my razor from my bag and cut his pant leg out of the bicycle sprocket to free him. He was relieved and grateful for my help.

As I looked at him, I realized he was shivering with cold, and his clothes were all wet. I immediately took off my coat and put it on him to keep him warm. The boy was now feeling better, but we needed to find his parents. I asked him where he lived, and he pointed towards a nearby house.

Years later, the same boy I had helped years ago, now a grown man with children, came forward to meet me. He reminded me of the incident and still thanked me for my help and told me that he still remembers that day very well. I was glad to have helped him.

Ironically, while I was helping him, an observer called the center and told them that a Brown truck driver had hit a child. This news spread like wildfire, and the incident went viral. However, all was cleared up, and there was a happy ending.

Love Valley is known for having some of the most beautiful and captivating places in town that are worth exploring. So, one day, while driving towards it on another usual day, my eyes caught sight of something lying on the side of the road. I stopped the truck and went a bit closer to inspect, in case it was something unusual.

I realized that it was a bank bag, and without any hesitation, I picked it up and placed it on the dashboard of my car. As I continued on my journey, my curiosity about what was inside the bag grew stronger. I couldn't resist the urge to peek inside, and to my surprise, there were a bunch of small bills amounting to $380 and a single check.

I realized that the bag belonged to someone, and I was determined to track down the owner. It turned out that a salesman had accidentally left the bag on the roof of his car and forgotten about it.

He was frantically searching for it and had gone everywhere to look for it. I knew that it was potentially a huge loss for him, especially since he was retired and on a fixed income. So, I decided to help him out. Using the information on the cheque, I was able to track down the owner and return the bag to him. The salesman was extremely grateful and couldn't thank me enough. He even wrote me a heartfelt note and gave me a $20 reward as a token of his appreciation.

As I sit at a higher height than most vehicles, I have the advantage of seeing things that others might miss. Over time, I have come across several items, such as pocketbooks, wallets, and even tools, that have been dropped or misplaced by their owners. I always make it a point to collect these items and try my best to return them to their rightful owners.

It is a small gesture, but it gives me immense satisfaction to know that I have been helpful in my own way. There have been times when it was challenging to identify the owners of these items, but I have never given up. I have used my resources, such as social media and community forums, to reach out to people and return their lost belongings.

It is a wonderful feeling to see the relief on the faces of people when they are reunited with their lost possessions.

And now, on a more sensitive matter, I have seen an amazing example of some people's sense of immodesty. I have had numerous women come to the door in various stages of undress, and I have seen some completely without clothes. One can never fully gauge the intentions of these women, but I try to remove myself from this situation as soon as possible. The consequences of such situations could really get out of hand quickly.

Regardless of what they had in mind, I have often thought much of this was for "shock value." And believe me, most of the drivers I know want to get out of there as soon as possible. I thought I had been propositioned on my route, and nothing was worth losing my job. As my dad always said, "Never get your honey where you get your money."

I just have to share this one story. A fellow driver was delivering a package for me. He came to the door, and a woman said she would be there in a minute. He waited five minutes. When she finally came to the door, she only had on underpants. To his surprise, she said, "Oh, you're not Scott," and slammed the door. I have had a lot of ribbing about this over the years.

On a more serious note, I have encountered a number of serious vehicle wrecks. One day, I came upon a homicide scene, and I knew all the parties involved. That package was not delivered that day. Also, I have thwarted some potential home invasions on my routes. As I would pull up to the house, I would see them leave immediately. It didn't take but a second to figure out what had happened.

CHAPTER 6
What Brown Done For Me

When those observing employees working at Brown wonder, 'Why do we work so conscientiously?'

My answer is, 'It's because Brown has escalated—in fact, magnified my life's objectivity to understand many probabilities to drastic development in every aspect of life.'

To be honest, Brown has not only transformed me into a better-skilled driver but, on personal grounds, has amplified my knowledge of almost every vehicle that I may come across. I have gained profound understanding, guidance, and expertise through Brown, which has helped me to navigate the roads with ease and interact with countless people along the way.

At Brown, we are constantly bombarded with safety habits and resources to secure ourselves along with others. May that even be, the life of an animal. Safety is the top priority for the entire Brown management. From the safety of the general public to our very own personal incidents, we are reminded to ensure emergency drills, safety seminars, and proactive steps are at the forefront of our business.

Brown has instilled in me a number of proficiencies throughout the years. The first I call is *"JOB NUMBER ONE."*

The main motive for writing this book is to share the depth of knowledge I have gained over the years. As an experienced driver, I have accumulated a wealth of knowledge about the ins and outs of driving safely on the road.

I have always been passionate about sharing this knowledge with others, but it wasn't until my son was approaching the age of getting his driver's license that I felt a sense of urgency to impart this information to him. I spent countless hours teaching him about the importance of defensive driving, how to stay alert on the road, and how to handle unexpected situations.

While I'm sure he may have grown tired of my constant reminders, I felt a great sense of relief when I saw that my teachings had finally sunk in and he was able to confidently pass his driver's test. Now, I feel compelled to share this depth of knowledge with others by writing this book in the hopes that it can help new drivers navigate the road safely and with confidence.

The whole idea is that in order to prevent an auto accident, it's important to maintain adequate space around your vehicle and ensure clear visibility while driving. To achieve this, there are five key habits that all drivers should adopt. These habits are commonly referred to as "seeing habits." To help remember them, Brown has come up with a simple mnemonic device: "All Good Kids Love Milk." Each letter in this phrase stands for one of the five habits:

"A" = Aim high in steering. How do you do this? You have an imaginary target, like a dart board. What does that do for you? It centers your vehicles in the traffic lane. It also gives you a safe path on turns. Here is a key phrase to remember. Visualize a safe path ahead.

"G"= Get the big picture. This one is my personal favorite. It's really all about space and visibility. How do you do this? How wide and deep is the road? What's in the road? Are the objects to avoid? What's the lay of the land? What does all do for you? For a start, it keeps you from being distracted. Always make smooth stops and turns. That buys time. Here's a key phrase. "Stay back and see it all."

"K" = Keep your eyes constantly moving. What a good way to do that! Keep your eyes to the front for two seconds and then to the rear every five to eight seconds. What does that do for you? It keeps you alive at intersections. It keeps your eyes ahead of your vehicles. Here is another key phrase. SCAN – don't STARE. Keep your eyes moving and not fixed with a constant stare forward.

"L" = Leave yourself an out. How do you do that? Always have an escape route. Take the path of least resistance. What does that do for you? It maintains space on all four sides of your vehicles – but always in front. Key phrase: Be prepared. Expect the unexpected.

"M" = Make sure the other driver sees you. How do you do that? You communicate in traffic. Use your horn, lights, and signals. On a personal note. My horn has saved me more than I can even remember. What does this do for you? It establishes "eye-to-eye" contact. Key phrase. Don't gamble – use your horn, light, and signals.

I would also like to share a 10-point commentary.

1. When stopped in traffic, have at least a car length in front of you.

Firstly, it's essential to maintain a safe distance from the vehicle in front of you, especially when stopped in traffic. You should have at least a car length between you and the car in front of you to allow for sudden stops or emergencies.

2. At all intersections, look left, right, and back left.

At intersections, it's crucial to look left, right, and back left before proceeding. This will help you avoid collisions with other vehicles, cyclists, or pedestrians.

3. Delay your start-up. Count "1, 2, 3."

When starting up, it's recommended that you hold on to your departure by counting "1, 2, 3." This brief pause will give you time to assess your surroundings and ensure that it's safe to proceed.

4. Following time – Anything under 30 mph, allow 4 to 6 seconds. Anything over 30 mph, allow 6 to 8 seconds.

When driving, you should always maintain a safe following distance. For speeds under 30 mph, it's recommended to allow 4 to 6 seconds of following time, and for speeds over 30 mph, 6 to 8 seconds.

5. Check your mirrors every 5 to 8 seconds.

Being attentive through your mirrors every 5 to 8 seconds is crucial to staying aware of your surroundings. It is important that this safety measure is to be implicated crucially.

6. Scan steering wheels. Look for signs of movement. This can help tremendously in parking lots, malls, and any other place where there are a lot of parked cars.

You should also scan steering wheels to look for signs of movement, which can be helpful in crowded areas such as parking lots or malls.

7. "Stale green light. Where a green light is getting ready to turn, make a set point of decision. Are you going through it, or are you going to stop?

When approaching a "stale green light" (a green light that's about to turn yellow), it's essential to make a set point of decision. You should decide whether you're going to proceed through the intersection or stop.

8. Always maintain an 8 to 12-second lead time from the vehicles in front of you.

It's recommended that you maintain an 8 to 12-second lead time from the vehicle in front of you to allow for sudden stops or changes in traffic.

9. When parked in a curve and pulling back out, always look over your left shoulder.

When parked in a curve and pulling out, always look over your left shoulder to ensure that it's safe to proceed.

10. Always make eye-to-eye contact.

Finally, it's essential to make eye contact with other drivers. This will help prevent miscommunications and misunderstandings, especially at intersections or when changing lanes.

I have jolted these details so that anyone reading them can avoid potential accidents. It would have been worth it if it could have saved even a single person from harm. Therefore, I urge you to share this valuable information with anyone who interacts with you and might benefit from it. Your act of sharing could make a significant difference in someone's life and keep them safe.

CHAPTER 7
Amazon! I Seen It Coming

Back in the day, when we used to sit together before the start of our workday, we would often engage in casual conversations about various topics. Topics that would draw us to contemplate and debate over hours of speculating. One such topic that frequently popped up was the stock market. We would discuss the prices of various stocks and, sometimes, share our opinions about which ones we thought were worth investing in.

I remember one particular day when the conversation had turned to the price of Brown stock. While everyone was sharing their thoughts and opinions, I spoke up and suggested that we should invest in Amazon.

At the time, Amazon was still a relatively new company, and many people were skeptical about its future potential. However, I had done my research and believed that Amazon had a bright future ahead. Unfortunately, despite my suggestion, we didn't take the opportunity seriously, and we missed out on a potentially profitable investment.

Looking back, I can't help but wonder what it would have been like if we had taken a chance on Amazon.

As a rural route driver, I had been noticing a steady and significant influx of packages being delivered to my customers. These packages, which were being ordered through Amazon, contained everything from daily essentials to special items that my customers may not have easy access to in their rural areas.

Electronic items, plastic products, and gadgets were frequently delivered in these areas, and Brown was delivering them. So, it was clear that many of my customers realized the convenience of having their purchases delivered directly to their doorstep rather than having to drive for miles to town to get them.

The impact of this shift in consumer behavior became noticeable in many various ways. For one, my delivery route changed dramatically, with many more stops to make along the way.

Surprisingly, I also gained new customers who appreciated the convenience of having their purchases delivered by me. Moreover, this trend helped me build stronger relationships with my existing customers, who now saw me as a trusted partner in their daily lives.

I was grateful for the opportunity to serve my customers in this way and was excited to see what the future holds for rural delivery services like mine.

Another big bang that was included in my route was the Union Grove. It was incorporated into my regular delivery route due to some additional stops that were added. At first, I wasn't quite sure what to expect from this area, but I must say that I ended up being pleasantly surprised as I began working alongside that. The community was charming and had a unique character that set it apart from other neighborhoods in the city.

As I made my way through the streets, I couldn't help but notice the rich history that was all around me.

For example, did you know that the name "Union" actually came from the fact that during the Civil War, Union soldiers were encamped there?

It's fascinating to think about how much has changed since then, yet how some things have remained the same. The Union Grove quickly became one of my favorite areas to deliver to, and with the strolling time, I always looked forward to my next visit with them.

Nestled in the heart of the southeastern United States, Union Grove is another charming town that boasts a vibrant cultural scene. Among its many attractions is the annual World Championship Fiddlers Convention, Older than the Grand Ole Opry, which became a celebrated event in the town's calendar.

This music festival, which has been running since 1924, enhanced in size and popularity over the years, drawing an impressive crowd of 100,000 people at its most recent event in 1980.

The World Championship Fiddlers Convention, older than the Grand Ole Opry, is a musical extravaganza that features an eclectic mix of genres, including country, bluegrass, rock, and pop. Attendees are expected to be dazzled by the performances of talented musicians and dancers from all around the world, showcasing their skills in a lively and festive atmosphere.

The festival was a true celebration of music, with banjos, guitars, and fiddles filling the air and the crowd swaying to the rhythm. In addition to the music, it was also a celebration of local food and drinks. Visitors indulged in a variety of delicious dishes, ranging from classic southern barbecue to mouth-watering seafood.

The opportunity to experience the warm hospitality of Union Grove with locals was incredible. The town was welcoming to visitors with open arms and made sure that everyone had a good time.

The World Championship Fiddlers Convention, older than the Grand Ole Opry, was a must-attend event for music lovers, and anyone looking to experience the rich culture and traditions of the southeastern United States was ecstatic to experience it. With its lively atmosphere, talented performers, and delicious food, it's no wonder that so many people flock to Union Grove every year to be part of this unforgettable festival.

Union Grove was once home to several dairy farms, which is a testament to my county's agricultural roots. It also boasts the highest number of dairy farms in the state; among my most cherished deliveries of Amazon package was Amazon Fire.

As one of Amazon's O.G. faces, I enjoyed delivering these packages; if I knew the customer well when delivering "Amazon fire," I would act like the package was burning my hands, and I had much fun with this!

Presently, while I sit here typing this chapter, I can hear the sound of an Amazon delivery truck pulling up outside near my backyard, and it seems that my wife has been their loyal Amazon Prime customer. Undoubtedly, she has been keeping the drivers super busy with at least three deliveries per week, and I have the pleasure of getting to know some of these delivery drivers who refer to themselves as "Oriners."

I have come across some really nice and hardworking young men and women who are just starting out on their journey in this field. When I see them hustling and bustling to complete their deliveries, it reminds me of my own early days when I first started working with Brown.

Despite the flurry of fuss, I appreciate Amazon's role in helping me get my message out to others, which is about the importance of safe driving. Moreover, it is substantial to believe that safe driving is crucial at every stage of life, and Amazon has been a great partner in raising awareness about this issue to countless individuals overall.

CHAPTER 8
Brown Preaches Safety

Every morning, at the PCM (pre-communication meeting) that we held, we made it a point to go over all the queries that we may have and have a detailed conversation on the safety tips for the day. This was a crucial session where we took the time to discuss doubts and plan how we could ensure a safe and secure work environment for all of our team members.

During this meeting, everyone had the opportunity to contribute and share their thoughts, ideas, and concerns with anyone they may have. We believe that every voice matters and that by working together, we can create a more informed and prepared Driver Group.

We also took the time to discuss past incidents or accidents that had occurred in the district and the current affairs that caused troubles. By doing so, we learned to put measures in place to prevent similar mishaps from happening in the future.

At Brown, understanding safety is taken very seriously, and at meetings like this, it is an essential part of our daily routine to keep everyone informed and updated on the latest safety protocols. We ensure that we are doing everything possible to prevent any potential hazards. Mostly, it seems that it is a "Welcome to my nightmare scenario." Like having maybe one of your worst days at Brown, openly discussed by the whole district.

For more than 18 years, I was a part of the Safety Committee at my workplace, which was responsible for ensuring the safety of our employees and customers. During this time, I had the opportunity to serve as an hourly co-chair, a position I held for many years before being appointed as a shop steward and a Safety co-chair. This being somewhat unusual.

As an hourly co-chair, I worked closely with other committee members to identify potential hazards and develop safety protocols to mitigate them. I was also responsible for conducting regular safety audits, which involved reviewing safety procedures and equipment and ensuring our employees were adequately trained to respond to emergency situations.

Later, as a shop steward and a safety co-chair, I was tasked with overseeing safety procedures in the workplace and ensuring that they were compliant with local and national regulations. I collaborated with other members of the committee to develop safety training programs and to implement safety policies that were effective in reducing the risk of accidents and injuries in the workplace.

Being an active safety committee, we met once a week to thoroughly discuss any and all safety concerns. Our focus was mainly on addressing problems that would arise within the terminals, particularly those that required immediate attention.

As the terminals were bustling with moving belts and rolling machinery, we would often share stories about the dangers and fatalities that could result from these hazards. These stories would serve as a reminder to all committee members that safety should always be a top priority.

To increase safety measures, we would often conduct demonstrations for drivers to ensure they were aware of the risks and how to mitigate them. Our main goal as a committee, however, was to raise awareness about safety and how it can positively impact everyone within the terminals.

As a member of the Safety Committee, my primary aim was to identify any potential safety issues and have them addressed before the next meeting. With all the moving belts and rolling safety inside the building, I could write some horror stories about ringing and death from these moving belts. This required a keen eye for detail and a willingness to take action, which was, by working together, we were able to create a safer working environment for everyone within the terminals.

Sometimes, we would clean all the drivers' windshields, thus showing them that we are an active committee. Once a year, we have an all-day safety conference with all committees in the division in attendance.

Here, we discuss things such as the most common accident at Brown, which is always backing the package car. Also, we discuss ways to possibly prevent accidents. We test the committee's knowledge and safety habits; if you don't know it, you can't teach it.

We come up with safety slogans and discuss safety protocols. One slogan I came up with is "Safety is no accident."

Think about it: If I use what I learned in my day, I feel fortunate for what I have learned and want to pass it on.

CHAPTER 9
Peak Season – O.G. Santa Claus

For thirty-four years, I have crisscrossed countless roads, delivering Christmas presents in a manner that often made me feel like Santa Claus. Each December, as the holiday spirit filled in every corner, I found myself occupied in the hustle and bustle of Peak Season at Brown. This period—the heart and soul of Brown—began right after Thanksgiving and extended until December 24. It was a time when all Brown employees showed their relentless dedication to the season's activities.

Peak season at Brown was a phenomenon in itself. It represented the pinnacle of our year, marked by a flood of packages and a solid commitment to ensuring every delivery reaches its destination right on time.

During the peak season, the usual rhythms of work-life balance are set aside. There are no vacations, no personal days, and falling ill is almost unthinkable. The stakes are so high, and the pressure is immense as the company ramps up operations to meet the heavy workload for holiday deliveries.

To handle the massive volume of packages, Brown hires a substantial number of additional staff. This includes not only extra drivers but also 100,000 helpers and additional inside help. These temporary employees are crucial to handling the increased workload and ensuring that every package reaches its destination on time. For many of these seasonal workers, this opportunity serves as a potential gateway into long-term employment with Brown, as their hard work and dedication are often noticed and rewarded.

The collaborative effort required during peak season is nothing short of extraordinary. The atmosphere is fully charged with a sense of urgency and camaraderie as everyone pulls together to achieve the common goal of delivering happiness to households everywhere.

In many ways, I see myself as a modern-day Santa Claus, but not in a red suit. Each package I deliver carries the promise of happiness, and I take great pride in being part of this grand tradition. As the days grow shorter and the nights longer, I go through my routes with the knowledge that my efforts contribute to the magic of the holiday season. This is peak season at Brown—a period of intense work, community spirit, and the profound satisfaction of knowing that, in my own way, I am bringing a bit of holiday cheer to the world.

It's no exaggeration that peak season at Brown is a whirlwind of activities and dedication, encompassing the period from Thanksgiving to December 24. This timeframe is marked by an intense focus on delivering an unprecedented volume of packages to meet the holiday demand. As soon as Thanksgiving passes, the entire operation shifts into high gear, and every day counts.

From Thanksgiving until Christmas Eve, the concept of vacations or personal days just vanished into thin air. The demands require all hands on deck, and the commitment to the job takes precedence over everything else. This period is not just another part of the year; it is the climax of our efforts, the moment when the true spirit and strength of Brown are showcased.

The volume of packages handled during Peak season is nothing short of record-breaking. Each year, the numbers seem to surpass the last, setting new benchmarks for efficiency and capacity. The sight of a fully loaded truck at the start of the day is both daunting and exhilarating.

My pre-loader often meets me before start time, and together, we marvel at the huge volume of parcels, usually only able to say, "Wow." We eagerly anticipate the sight of the truck filled to capacity. Despite the overwhelming load, by the end of the long, dark days, every package is delivered, confirming the collective effort and determination of everyone involved. The entire team comes together, driven by a shared goal of bringing holiday cheer to countless homes. The relentless pace and high stakes make it an unforgettable experience, year after year, showcasing the very best of what Brown can accomplish.

The daily routine during Peak season at Brown is a blend of routine tasks and unexpected challenges, demanding both physical endurance and mental agility. Each day begins with a familiar yet awe-inspiring ritual. The sheer of the packages is daunting, but it also serves as a powerful reminder of the importance of our mission during this crucial season.

I believe that delivering packages during peak season is more than just a job; it's a commitment to bringing fulfillment to families eagerly awaiting their holiday gifts. Each parcel represents a promise, and the importance of ensuring every package reaches its destination cannot be overstated. Whether it's a child's eagerly awaited toy or a heartfelt gift from a loved one, every delivery carries significant emotional weight. This understanding fuels our dedication and drives us to push through even the most exhausting days.

*   *   *

A key component of my role during peak season is mentoring the seasonal drivers who are hired specifically to help manage the holiday rush. They are often new to the fast-paced and demanding environment of package delivery. Despite their temporary status, Brown requires them to quickly learn and adhere to the safe driving methods and habits religiously followed at Brown.

So, each morning, before heading out on our routes, I spend time with the seasonal drivers, guiding them through the essential safety protocols and sharing practical tips for the day ahead.

Mentoring involves more than just imparting knowledge; it's about identifying and addressing any issues or problems that may arise. We review their past days' performance, pinpointing areas where they may have struggled and offering solutions to improve their efficiency and safety. Some seasonal drivers quickly realize that the demands of the job are not for them, and that's okay. The important thing is to ensure that those who stay are well-prepared and confident in their abilities.

Safe driving methods and habits at Brown are paramount during peak season, not only for the safety of the drivers but also for the timely delivery of packages. Each driver must understand and practice these methods to manage driving on busy roads and tight schedules effectively. This includes everything from defensive driving techniques to proper loading and unloading procedures. By emphasizing these safety practices, we aim to minimize accidents and ensure a smooth delivery process.

Identifying issues with seasonal drivers is an ongoing task. Some may struggle with the physical demands, others with the fast pace or the intricacies of going on unfamiliar routes. By closely monitoring their progress and providing continuous feedback, I help them overcome these challenges. It's about building their confidence and ensuring they feel supported in their roles.

*   *   *

The daily routine during peak season is intense and demanding, but it is also incredibly fulfilling. The challenges we face and overcome each day reinforce the importance of our work and the collective effort required to make the holiday season special for so many. Through mentorship, adherence to safety practices, and a shared commitment to excellence, we ensure that every package is delivered and every promise kept.

So, managing peak season at Brown requires a combination of strategic planning, adaptability, and community spirit. When the weather cooperates, with no snow or ice to impede our progress, operations can proceed relatively smoothly. Clear roads and mild weather conditions allow us to maintain a steady pace and meet our delivery targets with fewer disruptions. However, this is not always the case, and we must be prepared for whatever Mother Nature throws our way. Smooth operations are a team effort, requiring everyone to stay vigilant, efficient, and ready to face any possible issues.

The longevity of drivers at Brown is often measured by the number of "peak" seasons they have experienced. It's a unique metric that reflects not just their years of service but their endurance and resilience during the most demanding time of the year. Conversations among drivers often include references to how many peak seasons they have worked, serving as a badge of honor and their dedication. Each peak season adds to a driver's wealth of experience and reinforces their commitment to the job and the Brown community.

*　　　*　　　*

A cherished tradition during peak season is our visits to the local rest home to sing Christmas songs. These visits are a highlight, offering a welcome break from the daily grind and an opportunity to spread holiday happiness beyond the confines of our delivery routes.

A group of us, including drivers and other Brown employees, gather on a Saturday before Christmas to bring music and fun to the residents of the rest home. This experience is deeply moving for all of us. We see firsthand the happiness that our songs bring to the elderly residents.

Leading these musical visits is Retha, a driver's wife and a professional singer. Her leadership has been instrumental in making these events special. With her rich, melodious voice, she guides us through a repertoire of classic Christmas carols, setting the tone and lifting everyone's spirits. Her passion and professionalism inspire us all, and her presence ensures that our singing is not only heartfelt but also beautifully performed. She transforms these visits into memorable events that resonate deeply with both the residents and the participating drivers.

Rethera's leadership extends beyond just organizing and conducting the singing sessions. She connects with the residents, engaging them and encouraging them to join in the festivities. Her warmth and enthusiasm create an inclusive atmosphere where everyone feels valued and uplifted. These visits are more than just a performance; they are a shared celebration of the holiday spirit, bridging generations and bringing the community closer together.

As you can see, peak season is about more than just logistics and delivery metrics. For us, it involves developing a sense of camaraderie and community among the drivers, embracing traditions, and recognizing the dedication and resilience of the team.

Whether it's moving on clear roads, marking the passage of time through peak seasons, or singing Christmas songs under Retha's inspiring leadership, each element contributes to the successful management of this intense period.

So, community engagement is a cornerstone of our efforts. Beyond the rigorous demands of delivering packages, we take pride in our active participation in the communities we serve. This commitment is exemplified by our annual collection of gifts and our heartfelt interactions with the residents of the rest home.

Each year, as peak season nears, we organize a collection of gifts for the residents of this local rest home. This tradition has become a cherished part of our holiday activities. The drivers' group, along with the clerks and other staff, come together to contribute fruits, candy, nuts, and turkeys. We select gift items to bring comfort and pleasure to the elderly residents, many of whom reminisce about receiving similar treats in their childhood. The act of giving is deeply satisfying, reinforcing our bond with the community and reminding us of the true spirit of the holiday season.

As we gather, we sing Christmas songs for the residents. We perform in the common areas where residents can gather to enjoy the festive atmosphere.

For those who are unable to leave their rooms, we walk the halls, singing and bringing the holiday spirit directly to them. The appreciation and smiles on their faces are the most fulfilling feelings we could ask for.

These interactions are particularly meaningful to me, as I have been on the same route for 29 years. Over this time, many of the rest home residents have become more than just names and faces; many of them are my past customers and friends. The relationships built over nearly three decades are deep and lasting. Visiting them during the holidays feels like reconnecting with old friends and family. It's a chance to reminisce about shared experiences and to reinforce the bonds that make our community strong.

This community engagement, I believe, is about giving back to the communities that support us, building and nurturing relationships, and spreading love and respect during the holiday season. Through our collections of gifts, our singing visits, and our personal connections with residents and past customers, we strive to make a positive difference. These activities enrich our lives as much as those we serve, creating a sense of unity and shared purpose that defines the true spirit of the holidays.

*   *   *

Among the many traditions and activities, some events stand out as particularly memorable and heartwarming. One such event was Elvis's performance at the local rest home, an experience that left a lasting impact on both the residents and those of us who participated.

The idea to bring Elvis to the rest home was born out of a desire to do something extraordinary for the residents, many of whom had been loyal customers and friends for years. We wanted to create a unique and fun occasion that would brighten their holiday season in a way that mere gifts and songs couldn't. With that in mind, we arranged for an Elvis impersonator to put on a show.

So, one memorable year, I arranged for an Elvis impersonator to perform at the rest home. The residents were thrilled. Also, the performer was very dedicated and passionate and connected with the audience in a special way. His presence brought back fond memories and excited the residents. He was serious about it, naming his daughter Lisa Marie.

Dressed in a sparkling jumpsuit reminiscent of Elvis Presley's iconic stage attire, he was dedicated to his craft. His uncanny resemblance to the King of Rock' n' Roll, both in looks and voice, captivated the residents from the moment he stepped onto the makeshift stage in the rest home's common area. As he began to sing classics like "Hound Dog," "Love Me Tender," and "Jailhouse Rock," the atmosphere transformed. The residents, many of whom had grown up listening to Elvis, were transported back to a time filled with youthful memories and cherished moments.

One particularly poignant moment during the performance highlighted the profound impact of music and nostalgia. Among the audience was a former customer of mine, an elderly man suffering from Alzheimer's. His condition had left him largely unresponsive and disconnected from his surroundings. However, as Elvis sang "Can't Help Falling in Love," something incredible happened. The man's eyes lit up, and he began to move to the rhythm of the music. To everyone's surprise, he stood up and started dancing with remarkable grace and enthusiasm. His movements were fluid, and his face shone with a happiness that had been absent for much time.

The nurses and staff at the rest home were equally amazed. One nurse, who had cared for the man for years, commented that she had never seen him so animated and engaged. It was as if the music had unlocked a part of him that had been hidden away, bringing back the vitality and spirit of his younger days. The performance not only entertained but also provided a therapeutic experience, demonstrating the power of music to reach deep into the hearts and minds of those affected by memory loss.

This special event left a profound impression on all of us who witnessed it. It showed us the importance of going the extra mile to bring joy and comfort to those in our community, especially during the holiday season. The Elvis performance was more than just entertainment; it was a celebration of life, memory, and the enduring connections we share with the people we serve.

Reflecting on that day, I am reminded of the true essence of the holidays, i.e., creating moments of happiness that can touch lives in unexpected and meaningful ways. The sight of the residents singing along, clapping, and dancing with Elvis is etched in my mind for good.

*   *   *

I loved serving the residents of the rest home, and equally, I cared for our customers. Customer appreciation during Peak season is proof of the strong relationships and mutual respect that have developed over years of service. As drivers, we form bonds with the people on our routes, becoming familiar faces who bring more than just packages—we bring reliability, friendliness, and a personal touch. This connection becomes especially evident during the holiday season when our customers go out of their way to show their gratitude.

One of the most heartwarming aspects is the outpouring of appreciation from customers in the form of homemade treats and cash gifts. Throughout the month of December, my truck would often be laden not just with parcels but with an array of delicious baked goods—cookies, pies, cakes, and other festive treats. These homemade goodies are a labor of love, and receiving them is a highlight of the season. Each treat comes with a story, a tradition, and a personal connection, making them all the more special.

In addition to these delightful treats, many customers also express their gratitude through cash gifts. This tradition, though unexpected, is a humbling experience. I have often found myself handed an envelope with a heartfelt thank-you note and a monetary gift. These gestures are deeply appreciated, as they reflect the customers' recognition of the hard work and dedication that goes into ensuring their packages arrive on time.

Despite the generosity of these gifts, my initial reaction has always been to refuse them. I often tell my customers, "Look, you don't have to do this. I love serving you." For me, the best part of the job comes from the satisfaction of delivering smiles and making a difference in the community, not from receiving gifts. However, our customers are insistent. They appreciate the personal connection and the reliability we provide, and they want to show their gratitude in a tangible way.

Refusing these gifts can sometimes lead to a gentle but firm insistence from the customers. They genuinely want to give back and acknowledge the effort we put into our work. Over time, I have come to understand that accepting these gifts is also a way of honoring their appreciation and maintaining the strong bond we share. It's a reciprocal relationship where gratitude and respect flow both ways.

On Christmas Eve, the sense of appreciation reaches its peak. This is usually the last and one of the most intense days of deliveries before the holiday. Often, I am the last driver out, being on a rural route, the downtown routes usually finishing around lunchtime. This final push is filled with a mix of exhaustion and fulfillment, knowing that we have done our part to make the holidays special for so many families.

Customer appreciation shows the impact we have on the lives of those we serve. The homemade treats, cash gifts, and heartfelt gestures of gratitude make all the hard work worthwhile. They strengthen the bonds between us and our customers, turning routine deliveries into moments of mutual respect.

*   *   *

Christmas Eve is the final and most intense stretch of the peak season. It's a day filled with a sense of urgency, determination, and, ultimately, fulfillment. As one of the last drivers on the downtown routes, I find myself at the heart of the holiday hustle, ensuring that every last package reaches its destination before the celebrations begin.

Being the last driver out on a rural route is a unique experience. The streets, usually bustling with activity, are quieter as businesses close early and people retreat to their homes to prepare for the festivities. This tranquility contrasts sharply with the flurry of activity inside my truck, where each package represents a piece of someone's holiday joy. The sense of responsibility is immense, knowing that these final deliveries are crucial to completing the holiday magic for many families.

As the day progresses, the weight of the task at hand becomes more intense. Each stop is made with precision and care, ensuring that nothing is left behind. Despite the long hours and the physical toll, the spirit of Christmas keeps me going, driving me to make every delivery count.

One of the highlights of my Christmas Eve routine is the hospitality extended by the dairy farms on my route. These farms, a staple of the community, never close, even on the busiest days of the year. Their unwavering support and kindness provide a much-needed respite amid the hectic schedule. At the Piedmont Farm supply, I am often invited in for a meal, a gesture that speaks volumes about the close-knit relationships we have built over the years.

The meals at Piedmont Farm Supply are a comforting tradition. Knowing that I have a place where I can take a brief break and enjoy a home-cooked meal makes a world of difference. The farmers and their families treat me like one of their own, offering not just food but also a moment of warmth and friendship. Even on days when time is tight, they always save me a plate, ensuring that I don't miss out on their delicious hospitality.

These meals are more than just a chance to refuel; they demonstrate the community spirit that defines our work at Brown. Sitting down to eat, even for a short while, provides a moment of reflection and gratitude. It's a time to appreciate the connections we have forged and the mutual support that sustains us through the busiest season of the year. The laughter, the shared stories, and the simple act of breaking bread together are what make these moments so special.

As the final deliveries of the day are completed and the last packages are handed over, there is a profound sense of accomplishment. Christmas Eve may be the finale of peak season, but it is also a testament to the dedication, hard work, and community spirit that define our roles at Brown. The journey to this point has been challenging yet incredibly rewarding, and it's the support from customers and community members alike that makes it all worthwhile.

In the quiet moments after the last delivery, as I reflect on the day and the season as a whole, I am filled with a deep sense of fulfillment. The Christmas Eve routine, with its blend of intense work and heartfelt connections, captures the true essence of the holiday spirit. It is a time of giving, not just in the form of packages but also through the kindness, gratitude, and shared experiences that make this season so special.

* * *

As I told you earlier, many helpers are hired to manage workload during peak season. So, these helpers, often part-timers, play a crucial role in ensuring the smooth and efficient delivery of packages. For me, this experience is made even more special because many of my helpers are individuals I have known since their childhood.

Throughout the years, I have had the pleasure of working with numerous young helpers, some of whom grew up in the very communities I serve. Watching them evolve from curious kids into responsible, hardworking adults is a satisfying feeling. These part-timers bring energy, enthusiasm, and a fresh perspective to the job. Their familiarity with the area and its residents proves invaluable, enhancing our efficiency.

As a mentor, I take my responsibility toward these helpers very seriously. One of the ways I ensure they feel valued and appreciated is by treating them to breakfast and lunch. Starting the day with a hearty breakfast sets a positive tone, providing the energy and motivation needed for the long hours ahead. Whether it's a quick stop at a local diner or picking up some breakfast sandwiches on the go, this small gesture goes a long way in building morale and establishing a strong bond with my helpers.

Lunch is another opportunity to connect and show appreciation. Amidst the hustle and bustle of deliveries, we find moments to pause and enjoy a meal together. These breaks are more than just a chance to refuel; they are an opportunity to share stories, exchange laughs, and build a sense of teamwork. By treating my helpers to lunch, I aim to create a supportive and enjoyable working environment, reinforcing the idea that we are in this together as a team.

As the holiday season reaches its peak, the spirit of giving becomes even more pronounced. And I make it a point to get each of my helpers a Christmas gift. These gifts are tokens of appreciation for their hard work, dedication, and the invaluable support they provide. Whether it's a gift card, a small gadget, or something more personal, the goal is to show them that their contributions are recognized and valued. The delight and surprise on their faces—when they receive these gifts—are priceless, adding a festive touch to the demanding work we do.

The experience of working with driver helpers is one of collaboration, mentorship, and mutual respect. These helpers are not just temporary colleagues; they become an integral part of the Brown family, sharing in the challenges and triumphs of the season. The relationships built during this time often extend beyond the holiday rush, leaving lasting impressions on both the helpers and myself.

Sharing meals and giving Christmas gifts are just small ways to show appreciation, but they have a bigger impact. They help create a positive and supportive atmosphere where everyone feels valued and motivated. In the end, it's these gestures of kindness and recognition that boost overall efficiency. I recommend all the drivers out there to promote such an ambiance, and you will find it fulfilling.

* * *

Christmas Eve at Brown represents the pinnacle of our efforts during the peak season. It's a day charged with urgency and determination as we work tirelessly to ensure that every package reaches its destination before the holiday. The entire team comes together, often joined by support managers, to meet this critical deadline of delivering packages to a number of families awaiting their holiday deliveries.

Delivering packages on Christmas Eve requires a well-coordinated effort. The addition of support managers to the frontline team is crucial. These managers, who usually oversee operations from a higher level, step in to provide hands-on assistance and support. Their involvement in the all-hands-on-deck approach characterizes this day. They help address any issues that arise, from dealing with difficult routes to resolving logistical challenges, ensuring that the delivery process runs as smoothly as possible.

Support managers bring a wealth of experience and problem-solving skills, which are invaluable in handling the complexities of Christmas Eve deliveries. They assist in looking up bad addresses, rerouting packages if necessary, and providing real-time solutions to any obstacles that may delay deliveries. Their presence on the ground boosts morale and provides an additional layer of efficiency, helping drivers stay focused and on schedule.

The primary goal on Christmas Eve is clear—ensure that every package is delivered. This task, though straightforward in principle, involves meticulous planning and execution. The volume of packages is at its peak, and every minute counts. Drivers and support managers work in tandem, double-checking addresses, verifying delivery instructions, and making sure that no package is left behind. The sense of responsibility is immense, as each delivery is critical to fulfilling the holiday expectations of our customers.

One of the most challenging aspects of Christmas Eve deliveries is dealing with last-minute issues, such as packages with incomplete or incorrect addresses. Support managers play a crucial role in these situations, using their resources to quickly locate the correct information and reroute packages accordingly. This level of responsiveness is essential to ensure that even the most challenging deliveries are completed on time.

As Christmas Eve nears, the pressure mounts to complete the remaining deliveries. Every effort is made to overcome any remaining hurdles, from traffic delays to unforeseen complications. The collaborative spirit among drivers and support managers is in full swing.

The finale of our efforts is not just about fulfilling a professional obligation; it's about upholding the trust and expectations that our customers place in us. As the last package is handed over and the final route is completed, we reflect on the day's efforts with pride and a deep sense of accomplishment, knowing that we have brought a little more pleasure into the world… one package at a time.

During one peak season, my dedication to the job and commitment to seeing every package delivered was put to the ultimate test when I faced a severe health crisis. What began as an ordinary day quickly turned into a life-threatening situation when my colon burst, leading me to the emergency room.

The first signs of trouble were easy to dismiss. Feeling unwell was not uncommon during the intense demands, and I initially attributed my discomfort to the usual fatigue and stress. However, as the pain intensified and my condition worsened, it became clear that this was no ordinary health issue. Despite the increasing agony, I pushed through, driven by the need to fulfill my duties. By the time I sought medical attention, my skin had turned a troubling shade of yellow, indicating the severity of my condition.

When I finally made it to the emergency room, the diagnosis was both shocking and dire. My colon had burst, creating a hole in my bladder and causing a severe infection that left me septic. The doctors described me as a "walking dead man," emphasizing how critical my situation had become. Immediate emergency surgery was necessary to save my life.

The surgery itself was an ordeal. I underwent a colectomy, a procedure to remove the damaged portion of my colon, and spent the next two and a half weeks in the hospital. During this time, I lost 28 pounds, and my strength was sapped.

When I awoke from the surgery, I was greeted by the sight of both my managers standing by my bedside. Their presence provided much-needed comfort and encouragement during my recovery. I was actually overwhelmed with the visits from a sea of Brown shirts. It reminded me of the strong bonds we share in our Brown community.

One of my fellow drivers conveyed the gravity of my condition to others, saying, "If you want to see Scott, you better go." This statement showed how close I had come to not making it.

As I began the long road to recovery, I initially felt overwhelmed by the challenges ahead. I had never been this weak before, and the prospect of returning to my demanding job seemed daunting. However, my time on the cancer floor of the hospital offered a sobering perspective. Seeing patients in far worse conditions than mine inspired me to push through my recovery with determination and gratitude.

After months of physical therapy and gradual progress, I was finally ready to return to work ten months later. My recovery was made possible by my faith and the support of my personal savior. The journey back to health was tough, but it taught me invaluable lessons about resilience, perseverance, and the importance of taking care of oneself. The experience changed me, deepening my appreciation for life and the support network I had in my colleagues and community. I approached my work with renewed vigor and a sense of purpose, grateful for the opportunity to continue serving my customers and being part of the Brown family.

I realize how fortunate I am to have survived and regained my strength. The experience reinforced the importance of health and the power of community. It also made me realize the spirit of peak season at Brown, where dedication and support go hand in hand, enabling us to overcome even the most daunting obstacles.

*   *   *

As I reflect on my many years at Brown, the memories of peak season stand out as some of the most challenging yet rewarding times of my career. Each season was a journey of hard work and a shared sense of purpose. It is a time when the Brown family comes together, united by the goal of delivering holiday excitement to our customers. The experiences and memories created during this time are etched deeply into my heart.

From the pre-dawn start times to the late-night finishes, the physical and mental demands are intense. Yet, it is in these moments of pressure that we find our strength and solidarity. The sight of fully loaded trucks, the hustle and bustle of sorting centers, the smiles of customers receiving their much-anticipated packages—all these elements come together to create memories that define the essence of peak season.

One of my fondest memories is singing Christmas songs with my colleagues and the residents at the rest home; these moments of connection are the true spirit for me. Among the many songs we sing, my favorite has always been "Here Comes Santa Claus." This song, with its cheerful melody and festive lyrics, captures the excitement and magic of the holidays. Singing the familiar tune as we load our trucks and set out on our routes fills me with a sense of nostalgia and happiness.

As I go through the busiest time of the year, these memories and songs provide a source of motivation and inspiration. They remind me of the impact we drivers have on the lives of others and the importance of our role in making the holiday season special. The bonds we form with our colleagues, the gratitude we receive from our customers, and the personal satisfaction of a job well done are the true rewards.

These experiences have shaped me personally and professionally, reinforcing the values of perseverance, compassion, and the happiness of giving. I am grateful for the journeys and the memories

I made along the way. So, I see the peak season at Brown as a period of celebration of teamwork, dedication, and community spirit. The memories of these seasons are treasures that I will carry with me always.

CHAPTER 10
Being a Teamster

For 34 years, I proudly wore the mantle of a teamster. Those years were more than just a career; they were a significant part of my identity. The sense of pride I felt wasn't solely derived from the job itself but from being part of something larger—a movement, a brotherhood that stood for worker rights and unity.

Every day, I went to work with a deep sense of purpose, knowing I was contributing to a legacy of strength and solidarity that spanned generations. Reflecting back, I can see my tenure as a testimony to my commitment and resilience, mirroring the values that the Teamsters uphold.

Brotherhood and Commitment to Fellow Teamsters

The essence of being a Teamster lies in the unbreakable bond between its members. This brotherhood transcends mere workplace camaraderie;

it is a deep-seated commitment to one another's well-being, both on and off the job.

Over the years, I developed relationships with my fellow Teamsters that were akin to family ties. We supported each other through thick and thin, facing challenges collectively and celebrating victories as one. This mutual support system was crucial, especially during tough times like strikes or negotiations for various matters, especially our salaries. It fostered a culture where we looked out for each other, ensuring that no one stood alone in the face of adversity.

Joining the Teamsters was not a casual decision; it was a pledge to uphold the values and responsibilities that came with its membership. The oath taken upon joining it is a solemn promise to never bring reproach upon your brothers and to always act in the best interest of the collective. This oath is a cornerstone of the Teamster ethos, instilling a sense of duty and accountability in each member! It binds us to a higher standard of conduct, reinforcing our dedication to the principles of fairness, justice, and solidarity. By taking this oath, each member commits to the integrity of the union, ensuring that our actions always reflect the collective strength and honor of the Teamsters. It was a magnificent experience each time I reminisced.

My Role as a Shop Steward

Later, as a shop steward, one of my primary responsibilities was representing my fellow drivers during discipline hearings. This role was crucial because it ensured that every Teamster had a fair and just process when facing allegations or disciplinary actions.

My goal was to advocate for the rights of my colleagues, ensuring that management followed proper procedures and respected the terms of our contract. Each hearing was an opportunity to defend the integrity and dignity of our members, emphasizing the importance of fair treatment. By standing up for my fellow Teamsters, I helped maintain a workplace where justice and respect were paramount.

Gary: My Fellow Steward

Collaboration was at the heart of my work as a shop steward, and my partnership with fellow steward,

Gary, was vital to our success. Together, we formed a dynamic team, combining our strengths and experiences to effectively represent our members.

Gary and I worked closely to strategize and prepare for hearings, ensuring we presented a united front. Our shared commitment to the well-being of our fellow Teamsters fostered a strong sense of teamwork and mutual respect. By working together, we tackled complex issues effectively, leveraging our combined knowledge and skills to achieve the best outcomes for our members.

Settling grievances, terminations, and other workplace issues was a significant aspect of my role as a shop steward. Gary and I dedicated ourselves to resolving these matters swiftly and fairly, always prioritizing the interests of our members. Whether it was negotiating with management to overturn an unjust termination or addressing day-to-day grievances, we ensured that the rights of Teamsters were upheld.

We approached each case with diligence and determination, understanding that our efforts directly impacted the lives and livelihoods of our colleagues. By successfully handling all these challenges, we helped foster a fairer and more equitable work environment, reinforcing the principles of solidarity and justice that define the Teamsters.

Management Adherence

The contract, often referred to as our "bible," was the foundation upon which our rights and responsibilities were built. As a shop steward, it was my duty to ensure that management adhered to every clause and stipulation within this vital document.

The contract delineated the terms of employment, including wages, benefits, working conditions, and dispute resolution procedures. By rigorously enforcing the contract, we safeguarded the protections it provided and ensured that management could not deviate from agreed-upon practices.

Ensuring adherence required constant vigilance and a thorough understanding of the contract's provisions. It involved regular communication with management to remind them of their obligations and to challenge any attempts to undermine the contract.

By holding management accountable, we maintained the integrity of our agreements and protected the interests of all Teamsters. This diligent oversight was crucial in preventing abuses of power and ensuring a fair and equitable workplace for everyone.

The Strike of 1997

The strike of 1997 was a pivotal moment in our history as Teamsters. For two and a half weeks, operations at Brown came to a complete standstill, demonstrating the immense power and solidarity of our union.

This strike was not merely a work stoppage; it was a bold assertion of our rights and a clear message to management about the strength and unity of the Teamsters. The impact of the strike was profound, affecting not only the company's operations but also highlighting the critical role that our members played in the company's success. It was a period marked by tension, resilience, and an unwavering commitment to our collective cause.

The significance of the 1997 strike was further amplified by the substantial contract that was subsequently signed. This new agreement addressed many of the key issues that had led to the strike, offering improved terms and conditions for our members.

Given the breadth and depth of this contract, there was a prevailing sense that this might be the last strike for Brown for the foreseeable future. The new contract was designed to provide long-term stability and minimize the likelihood of future disputes escalating to the point of a strike. It represented a major victory for the Teamsters, securing critical gains and setting a new standard for our working conditions.

The success of the strike was not solely due to our actions on the picket lines but also to the meticulous preparations that took place beforehand. These preparations were crucial in ensuring that we were ready for the challenges ahead.

In the lead-up to the strike, Gary and I made regular visits to the Union Hall. These visits were essential for staying informed about the ongoing contract negotiations and the broader strategy of the union. By attending meetings and discussions, we were able to gather critical information and insights that we could share with our fellow drivers. This direct line of communication with union leadership helped us stay aligned with the overall objectives and prepared for any developments.

Effective communication with our drivers' group was another key component of our pre-strike preparations. Gary and I took it upon ourselves to keep our fellow Teamsters informed about the status of negotiations and the potential for a strike.

We held meetings, distributed updates, and made sure that everyone understood the importance of unity and solidarity. This constant communication helped build a sense of collective resolve and ensured that everyone was on the same page.

One of the practical steps we took was encouraging our members to build personal strike funds. Understanding the financial strain that a strike could impose, we advised our fellow drivers to start setting aside money well in advance. This step was crucial for ensuring that our members could sustain themselves and their families during the strike. This way, we mitigated some of the financial pressures and helped maintain morale and commitment throughout the duration of the strike.

The strike of 1997 was living proof of the power of preparation, solidarity, and collective action. Our efforts laid the groundwork for the resilience and determination we displayed on the picket lines, ultimately leading to a significant victory for the Teamsters.

Meeting and Campaigning for Ron Carey

Meeting Ron Carey was a defining moment in my career as a Teamster. As a former Brown driver who had risen through the ranks to become the President of the Union, Carey embodied the values and spirit of our brotherhood.

I first met Ron Carey during one of his campaign rallies, where his passion and commitment to the union's cause were evident. His speeches resonated with many of us, inspiring confidence in his leadership and vision for the future.

Campaigning for Ron Carey was an experience that deepened my understanding of union dynamics and the importance of strong leadership.

Alongside other dedicated Teamsters, I canvassed for support, engaged in discussions with fellow members, and promoted Carey's candidacy. This grassroots effort was instrumental in building momentum for his election and highlighted the collective power of our membership.

Carey's Legacy as an Honest Union President

Ron Carey's tenure as union president left a firm mark on the Teamsters. Known for his integrity and unwavering dedication to our cause, his leadership was characterized by transparency, accountability, and a deep respect for the members he represented. Unlike some leaders who might be tempted by personal gain or external pressures, Carey remained steadfast in his commitment to the principles of fairness and justice.

His legacy as one of the most honest presidents in the union's history was cemented through his actions and decisions. Carey was not afraid to stand up to management. He ensured that our contract rights were upheld and that the voices of the workers were heard every time.

His honesty and straightforward approach earned him the trust and admiration of the Teamsters, and it also grew a culture of mutual respect and solidarity within the union. Carey's leadership style not only strengthened our resolve but also reinforced the core values that define what it means to be a Teamster.

Instructions During the Strike Call

When the decision to strike was made, Ron Carey's leadership was pivotal in guiding us through the challenging period. His clear and decisive instructions during the strike call were crucial in mobilizing our efforts and maintaining unity. He emphasized solidarity and discipline, instructing us to adhere strictly to the set protocols and to support one another throughout the process.

Carey's guidance included practical steps, such as organizing strike lines and ensuring that every member knew their role and responsibilities. He personally communicated the need for everyone to report to the strike line, sign up for shifts, and maintain a visible and united presence. His instructions were not just about logistics; they were also about instilling a sense of purpose and resolve among the members. By dividing the driver group and coordinating our efforts, we were able to present a cohesive front that demonstrated our collective strength.

Ron Carey's leadership and influence were defining factors in my experience as a Teamster. His commitment to honesty, integrity, and effective leadership left a lasting impact on the union and its members, setting a high standard for future leaders to follow.

Lessons Learned from the Strike

The strike of 1997 was not only a period of intense action but also a revealing time for understanding our members' behaviors and attitudes.

Throughout the strike, I gained valuable insights into my fellow Teamsters' diverse motivations, strengths, and weaknesses. Some members who had previously been quiet or unassuming stepped up in remarkable ways, showing leadership, resilience, and dedication that I hadn't seen before. These pleasant surprises highlighted the hidden strengths within our ranks and reinforced the importance of unity and collective action.

Conversely, the strike also exposed areas where our support and solidarity needed to be strengthened. Some members struggled with the financial and emotional strain of the strike, and it became clear that not everyone was equally prepared for the challenges we faced.

These observations showed us the necessity of thorough preparation and ongoing support for all members, ensuring that everyone was equipped to handle the pressures of collective action. Overall, the strike provided a deeper understanding of our membership and the critical role that each individual played in the success of our union efforts.

Our strike line received high praise from various quarters, and this recognition was a source of immense pride for all of us involved. Organized, disciplined, and highly visible, our strike line became a model for other groups within the district. We were commended for our commitment to maintaining a strong and united front, which was instrumental in applying pressure on the management and showcasing our solidarity.

The effectiveness of our strike line was not merely about numbers but also about the quality of our presence. We ensured that the strike line was well-staffed at all times, with members rotating in shifts to maintain a constant and energetic presence.

Military-Style Management of the Strike Line

Gary and I, being veterans, brought a military-style approach to managing the strike line. This management style proved to be highly effective in maintaining order, discipline, and efficiency. We applied principles of military organization to ensure that every aspect of the strike line was meticulously planned and executed.

From the outset, we established clear roles and responsibilities, ensuring that every member knew their duties and the importance of their contributions. We implemented a structured schedule for shifts, ensuring that the strike line was always well-staffed and that members had ample rest periods. This approach helped prevent burnout and maintained high energy levels throughout the strike.

In addition to logistical planning, we also emphasized the importance of morale and camaraderie. We encouraged team-building activities, regular briefings, and open communication to keep spirits high and ensure that everyone felt involved and informed.

Our military-style management not only enhanced the effectiveness of our strike line but also nurtured a sense of unity and shared purpose among the members.

The lessons learned from the strike of 1997 were invaluable. The insights into member behaviors, the high praise for our strike line, and the successful implementation of military-style management all contributed to a deeper understanding of what it takes to organize and sustain a successful strike. These experiences reinforced the importance of preparation, discipline, and solidarity in achieving our collective goals as Teamsters.

Challenges and Confrontations

During the strike, one of the most significant challenges we faced was the direct confrontation with division managers. Tensions were high as management attempted to undermine our efforts and pressure us back to work. One particular encounter stands out in my memory when the division manager, accompanied by two other managers, visited our strike line. Their presence was intended to intimidate us, but instead, it strengthened our resolve.

I confronted the division manager directly, expressing the frustrations and anger that many of us felt. I said to him, "If Jim Casey (one of our revered founders) were still alive, he would have fired all three of you for your actions."

This bold statement was a reflection of the deep-seated loyalty and respect we had for the principles upon which our union was built. It was a tense moment, but it was necessary to demonstrate that we would not be easily intimidated or swayed from our course.

Post-strike Conversations with Center Manager

After the strike was settled, the atmosphere remained charged with unresolved tensions. My center manager approached me, bringing up the division manager's lingering displeasure with our previous conversations. It was clear that my outspoken stance during the strike had left a lasting impression, and I was now marked as a troublemaker in the eyes of some in management. The center manager's words were a thinly veiled warning, suggesting that my job security was in jeopardy.

In response, I made it clear that I was not afraid of the consequences. I told him, "You can't eat me. All you can do is fire me, and if I don't do anything stupid, I will get my job back with back pay."

This statement showed my unwavering resolve and my deep understanding of the protections afforded to us by our contract. It was a reminder that our rights were not easily trampled upon and that we had the means to defend ourselves against unjust actions.

The challenges and confrontations I faced during and after the strike had a deep and long-term impact on my career and personal resolve. Being targeted by management for my outspoken stance was not an easy position to be in, but it reinforced my commitment to the principles of solidarity and justice. I learned that standing up for what is right often comes with significant personal risks, but it is a necessary part of being a leader and a steward of the union.

This period also strengthened my resolve to continue fighting for the rights of my fellow Teamsters. The experiences of the strike and its aftermath were powerful reminders of the importance of resilience and determination.

I became more vigilant and proactive in my role, ensuring that management adhered to our contract and that our members were protected from unfair treatment.

The lessons learned during these confrontations helped shape my approach to leadership, emphasizing the need for courage, integrity, and an unwavering commitment to the collective good.

Cherishing Teamster Brotherhood

One of the most rewarding aspects of being a Teamster was celebrating the victories we achieved together, particularly the reinstatement of fired drivers. Each time a driver who had been unjustly terminated was brought back to work, it felt like a personal triumph for all of us. These victories were not just about restoring jobs; they were about upholding justice and ensuring that our rights were respected.

I vividly remember the satisfaction of calling a fired driver to tell them they could return to work. The relief and gratitude in their voice were intense. These moments served as reminders of why we fought so hard and why our unity was so crucial. Celebrating these victories strengthened our bond and reaffirmed our commitment to each other.

Importance of Strong Members to Compensate for Weaker Ones

The strength of the Teamsters lay in our collective power, but within that collective, it was essential to have strong members who could lead and support those who were less resilient.

Throughout my years as a Teamster, I witnessed the critical role that strong members played in maintaining the integrity and effectiveness of our union. These individuals often stepped up during challenging times, providing leadership, courage, and a sense of direction for others to follow.

Having strong members to compensate for weaker ones ensured that we could get through difficult times without losing our momentum. These strong members were not just physically present but were also emotionally and intellectually committed to our cause. They inspired others, helped boost morale, and provided the necessary backbone when times got tough. Their strength was a key factor in our ability to achieve our goals and protect our members' rights. Recognizing and nurturing this strength within our ranks was crucial for the sustained success of the union.

Building Lasting Relationships and Camaraderie

One of the most enduring benefits of being a Teamster was the lasting relationships and camaraderie that were built over the years. The bonds formed through shared experiences, both challenging and rewarding, created a deep sense of brotherhood that went beyond the workplace. These relationships were characterized by mutual respect, trust, and a genuine concern for each other's well-being.

The camaraderie among Teamsters was evident in the small acts of kindness and support that were part of our daily interactions. Whether it was covering a shift for a colleague in need, standing together on the picket line, or simply sharing a meal and conversation, these moments fostered a sense of belonging and community. The friendships I developed as a Teamster have lasted a lifetime, providing a network of support that extends far beyond our professional lives.

Building these lasting relationships required effort and a commitment to the principles of solidarity and mutual aid. It involved being there for one another in times of need and celebrating together in times of joy. The sense of brotherhood that developed was a source of our strength and comfort. We knew full well that we were never alone in our struggles or our successes.

Strength of Organized Labor

The strength of organized labor, particularly within the Teamsters, was a daunting force in New York and beyond. Our influence extended far beyond the confines of individual workplaces, impacting broader labor policies, industry standards, and even political landscapes. The Teamsters were known for their ability to mobilize large numbers of workers, leverage collective bargaining power, and effect significant changes that benefited not only their members but also the wider labor community.

In New York, the presence of the Teamsters was especially pronounced. The city, with its dense concentration of industries reliant on logistics, transportation, and delivery services, provided a powerful platform for our union's activities.

Our ability to organize strikes, negotiate favorable contracts, and advocate for workers' rights made us a key player in the labor movement. The reputation of the Teamsters as a strong, united, and effective union was well-known, and it commanded respect from both employers and policymakers.

Beyond New York, the Teamsters' influence was felt nationwide. Our successful negotiations set precedents that often trickled down to other unions and industries. For example, when Brown drivers secured wage increases or improved working conditions, these gains often influenced similar negotiations in other sectors. The ripple effect of our victories demonstrated the far-reaching power of organized labor and the importance of solidarity among workers across different industries and regions.

Hoffa's Leadership Style and Legacy

Jimmy Hoffa Jr. carried a significant legacy as the son of one of the most famous labor leaders in American history, and his leadership style reflected his father's influence and his own vision. His approach was marked by a combination of strategic acumen, unwavering determination, and a deep commitment to the rights and welfare of union members.

Hoffa's leadership style was characterized by his ability to tackle complex negotiations with a blend of toughness and diplomacy. He was known for his willingness to stand firm on critical issues while also being able to engage in constructive dialogue with employers. This balance allowed him to secure significant victories, maintaining the respect of both union members and management.

Hoffa Jr. emphasized the importance of unity and solidarity and encouraged members to collaborate toward common goals. His efforts to modernize the union and adapt to changing industry landscapes helped ensure that the Teamsters remained relevant and effective in advocating for workers' rights. Hoffa Jr.'s legacy is one of strengthening the union's foundations and expanding its influence.

One of the most tangible impacts of Hoffa's leadership was seen in the improved conditions for truck drivers. He led numerous negotiations that resulted in better wages, benefits, and working conditions for drivers, directly affecting their daily lives and long-term job satisfaction. These negotiations were not merely about incremental gains but often involved substantial improvements that set new standards in the industry.

For example, Hoffa Jr. secured contracts that addressed critical issues such as job security, health and safety standards, and pension benefits. These victories meant that truck drivers could work with greater peace of mind, knowing that their livelihoods were protected and that they had a robust support system in place. The improved wages and benefits also helped attract and retain talent within the industry, ensuring a stable and skilled workforce.

The Evolution and Patriotism of Teamsters

The history of the Teamsters is rich with stories of struggle, resilience, and triumph. Since its inception over a century ago, the union has been at the forefront of the labor movement, advocating for workers' rights and better working conditions. The early years of the Teamsters were marked by significant challenges, including violent confrontations with employers and law enforcement. Many of the first Teamsters were met with fierce opposition as they fought to establish the union and protect their members.

One of the most poignant chapters in Teamster's history involves the sacrifices made by its members in the face of such adversity. Several Teamsters lost their lives during strikes and labor disputes, murdered by company thugs and anti-union forces. These early struggles were pivotal in galvanizing the union's resolve and commitment to its cause. The determination and bravery of these early members laid the foundation for the union's future successes.

As the union grew, so did its influence and capacity to secure significant victories for its members. The Teamsters played a crucial role in negotiating better wages, safer working conditions, and comprehensive benefits for workers across various industries. Each triumph was a result of collective action and the steadfast spirit of the union. The historical context of the Teamsters is a story of perseverance against the odds, showcasing the union's evolution from a fledgling organization to a powerful advocate for labor rights.

Commitment to Patriotism and Non-Violence at Rallies

Patriotism is a deeply ingrained value among Teamsters, reflecting their commitment to the principles of democracy, freedom, and justice. This sense of patriotism is evident in the union's activities and the conduct of its members, particularly during rallies and demonstrations. Unlike some labor movements that have been associated with violent protests, the Teamsters have consistently emphasized the importance of non-violence and respect for the law.

The commitment to non-violence is rooted in the belief that true strength comes from unity and moral integrity, not from physical confrontation. During rallies, Teamsters demonstrate their solidarity through peaceful protests, making their voices heard while maintaining order and discipline. This approach not only ensures the safety of all participants but also garners public support and respect for the union's cause. The orderly conduct of Teamster rallies stands as the union's dedication to achieving its goals through peaceful means.

Moreover, the patriotism of the Teamsters is reflected in their respect for national symbols and traditions. At Teamster rallies, the American flag is prominently displayed, and acts of disrespect, such as flag burning or destruction, are strictly prohibited. This respect for the flag symbolizes the union's appreciation for the country and the democratic principles that allow for the existence and flourishing of labor movements. The Teamsters view their fight for workers' rights as part of a broader commitment to the American ideals of fairness, justice, and opportunity for all.

Pride and Legacy of Being a Teamster

Being a Teamster is more than just a job; it is a source of immense pride and a legacy that spans over a century of labor advocacy. The journey of the Teamsters is marked by resilience, unity, and a commitment to workers' rights. This legacy is built on the sacrifices and triumphs of countless members who have stood together in the face of adversity, fought for fair treatment, and achieved significant victories that have shaped the labor landscape.

The pride of being a Teamster comes from belonging to a brotherhood that values solidarity and mutual support. It is a pride that stems from knowing that we are part of a powerful movement that has consistently championed the cause of workers, ensuring that their voices are heard and their rights are protected.

Reflecting on my personal journey as a Teamster, I am filled with a sense of accomplishment and gratitude. Over the years, I have had the privilege of representing my fellow drivers, standing up for their rights, and contributing to meaningful changes that have improved our working conditions.

The collective achievements of the Teamsters are a source of inspiration and remind us of what can be accomplished when we stand together. From historic strikes to groundbreaking negotiations, the successes of the union have had far-reaching impacts, not only for its members but for the broader labor movement. These achievements have set new standards in the industry, improved the lives of countless workers, and demonstrated the enduring power of organized labor.

The challenges we face may evolve, but the principles that guide us remain constant. Through personal and collective achievements, we have demonstrated the power of solidarity and standing together in pursuit of common goals.

As we look to the future, we carry forward the lessons and values that have defined our union, confident in our ability to continue making a positive impact and advancing the cause of workers' rights.

CHAPTER 11
A Driver's Typical Day

Life as a package delivery driver has been a unique combination of independence, responsibility, and constant motion. Every day brings new challenges and opportunities, making it a job unlike any other. From the moment the driver leaves the terminal, they are on their own, going on a carefully planned route, managing time, and ensuring that every package reaches its destination.

A delivery driver's day starts around 8:30 am. They begin by loading their truck with their next-day air Packages, each one promising timely delivery. The process requires meticulous attention to detail; a single misloaded package can disrupt the entire day. The real journey begins once the truck is loaded and the driver leaves the terminal.

The independence of a delivery driver is both exhilarating and daunting. Without a supervisor constantly looking over their shoulder, drivers must rely on their own skills and judgment to get the job done.

This autonomy is one of the most appealing aspects of the job for many drivers, offering a sense of freedom that is rare in many other professions. However, with this freedom comes some serious responsibility.

Once the driver leaves the terminal, they face numerous challenges. Rural routes can span 160 to 180 miles, requiring the driver to go through remote areas often lacking clear signage or landmarks.

Urban routes, on the other hand, present their own set of obstacles, such as heavy traffic, limited parking, and frequent stops. Regardless of the route, time management is crucial. Delivering a package late can result in warnings or even more severe consequences. Thus, making punctuality a top priority is not a choice.

Drivers must also be prepared for the unexpected. Whether it's dealing with misloaded packages, encountering hazardous materials, or facing adverse weather conditions, the ability to adapt and think on their feet is essential. The job demands physical endurance, as drivers often walk several miles a day and handle heavy packages. Mental resilience is equally important, as they must stay focused and calm despite tight schedules and constant monitoring.

Despite these challenges, many drivers find immense satisfaction in their work. The sense of accomplishment from delivering every package on time, the appreciation from customers, and the freedom of being on the road make it a rewarding career.

The life of a delivery driver is a blend of balance, independence, and responsibility, showcasing the dedication and hard work that goes into ensuring that packages arrive at their destinations safely and timely.

A delivery driver's day begins with a critical task: delivering the Next Day Air Packages, often marked for Next Day Air service. This initial delivery is of utmost importance, as it sets the tone for the rest of the day. The Next Day Air package typically contains time-sensitive items, ranging from essential documents to perishable goods, which must reach their destination without delay.

Once the driver leaves the terminal, the clock starts ticking. The urgency of the Next Day Air package requires the driver to be swift and meticulous. This delivery often takes precedence over other tasks, highlighting the driver's ability to prioritize and manage time effectively.

Rural Routes and the Distances Covered

Rural routes pose a unique set of challenges for delivery drivers. Unlike urban areas, where stops are frequent and distances short, rural routes can span vast distances, sometimes 5 TO 10 miles between deliveries. These routes take drivers through remote and often picturesque landscapes, from winding country roads to expansive farmlands.

Traveling on rural routes requires a keen sense of direction and familiarity with the area. GPS devices may not always be reliable in these regions, making the driver's knowledge and experience invaluable. The isolation of rural routes means that a driver must be self-sufficient and able to handle any issues that arise without immediate assistance.

In addition to the long distances, rural routes often involve fewer but larger deliveries. This can mean transporting heavier packages, such as agricultural supplies or equipment, which adds a physical component to the job. The driver must balance speed with caution so that each package is delivered safely.

Consequences of Late Deliveries

A single delayed delivery can cascade into a series of setbacks, affecting the driver's entire schedule for the day. The consequences are more than just logistical; they also have professional implications. Drivers who consistently deliver packages late are subject to office visits and reprimands. These meetings can range from a simple discussion to more formal disciplinary actions, depending on the frequency and severity of the delays.

Being called into the office for a late delivery is a dreaded experience for any driver. It not only disrupts their day but also adds stress and pressure to an already demanding job.

For many drivers, the key to avoiding these consequences lies in meticulous planning and adaptability. They must be able to think on their feet, find the quickest and most efficient routes, and make adjustments on the fly. This ability to manage time and prioritize tasks is what separates successful drivers from those who struggle.

Getting Back on Track

After completing the initial task of delivering the Next Day Air package, the delivery driver must quickly transition back to their designed route, known as "Trace." This route is meticulously planned to maximize efficiency and minimize travel time between stops. Returning to Trace after the initial deliveries is crucial for maintaining the overall schedule.

Reintegrating into the designed route requires a seamless shift in focus. The driver must immediately align their actions with the pre-planned path, ensuring that every subsequent stop is executed with precision. This phase of the day emphasizes the importance of strategic thinking and adaptability, as the driver must balance the rigidity of the planned route with the flexibility needed to handle unforeseen circumstances.

A key aspect of a delivery driver's day is "reaching the shelf," which refers to the stage where the driver can operate efficiently without major disruptions and be able to walk inside the truck. Achieving this state is akin to finding a rhythm, where each delivery flows smoothly into the next, minimizing downtime and maximizing productivity.

Maintaining purity in the routine is essential. This purity signifies a day free from significant issues such as misplaced packages, mechanical failures, or route deviations. When a driver reaches this level of efficiency, their day becomes more manageable and predictable. The ability to maintain a pure routine reduces stress and enhances performance, making the driver more effective and reliable.

Challenges Like Unloading Parts of the Truck for Specific Stops

Despite careful planning, drivers often face the challenge of unloading parts of the truck to access specific packages. This task can be physically demanding and time-consuming. For instance, a package needed at the next stop might be buried under several others, requiring the driver to temporarily unload and reload the truck.

These interruptions demand quick thinking and physical agility. The driver must balance the need for speed with the necessity of handling packages carefully to avoid damage. Each instance of unloading and reloading adds to the day's physical toll.

The Urgency and Constant Movement

The life of a delivery driver is defined by urgency and constant movement. Every moment counts, and there is little room for error or delay. Drivers must be in perpetual motion, going through traffic, handling packages, and making deliveries with care.

The urgency of the job is driven by tight schedules and high expectations. Customers rely on timely deliveries, and any delay can lead to dissatisfaction and potential repercussions for the driver. This pressure necessitates a relentless pace, where every action is executed with a sense of immediacy.

The constant movement also means that drivers must be physically fit and mentally sharp. The demands of the job require a high level of stamina and the ability to stay focused throughout long hours on the road. They must be adept at multitasking, managing both the physical aspects of handling packages and the cognitive demands of time management.

Urban Vs. Rural Routes

The "Concrete Jungle" is a term often used to describe the densely packed, bustling urban areas where delivery drivers face unique and intense challenges. In the city, drivers go through a maze of traffic, one-way streets, and limited parking. The urban environment is characterized by constant noise, congestion, and a high volume of stops, making the job both physically and mentally demanding.

Delivering in the Concrete Jungle requires drivers to be quick and efficient. They must manage tight schedules, often making numerous stops within a small geographic area. The pressure to deliver on time is immense, and the slightest delay can cause a ripple effect. Additionally, drivers must deal with impatient motorists, crowded sidewalks, and frequent interruptions.

The pace of work on rural routes differs from that in the city. While the distances are longer, the stops are fewer, allowing drivers to spend more time on the road, what we call "Wind Shield Time." This can create a sense of solitude and peace as drivers are away from the constant noise and activity of urban environments. However, the isolation also means that drivers must be self-reliant, as help may not be readily available in remote areas.

Personal Experiences of Working in the "Concrete Jungle" and Transitioning to a Rural Route

My career began in the Concrete Jungle, where I spent the first four years dealing with the complexities of urban delivery. The relentless pace and constant challenges were overwhelming at times. I remember feeling possessed by the devil during those years as I jumped off docks and ran through crowded streets, often never finding the stairs. My customers affectionately called me "Wildman" because of my frenzied pace and determination to complete my deliveries.

Transitioning to a rural route after those intense years was a significant change. My life transformed as I moved from the city's chaos to the countryside's tranquility.

I found a new rhythm on my rural routes, which I had for twenty-nine years. The open roads, the peaceful surroundings, and the longer stretches between stops brought a sense of calm and balance to my work. This change not only improved my professional life but also profoundly impacted my personal well-being.

The environment in which a driver works impacts their life and career. Urban routes can lead to burnout and stress. The physical toll of going through traffic, handling numerous packages, and dealing with the chaos of the city can be exhausting. This fast-paced environment can be exhilarating for those who thrive on adrenaline and enjoy the dynamic nature of city life.

Drivers on rural routes often develop a deep connection with their surroundings and the communities they serve. The longer distances and fewer stops allow for a more thoughtful and deliberate approach to deliveries.

Both environments have their unique challenges and rewards. The Concrete Jungle tests a driver's agility, speed, and ability to handle stress, while rural routes demand self-reliance, endurance, and an appreciation for solitude. The choice between the two often comes down to personal preference and the kind of lifestyle a driver wishes to lead.

Night Deliveries and Safety

Working late into the night is a common reality, especially during the winter months when daylight hours are shorter. The shift from daylight to darkness brings a new set of challenges and requires heightened awareness and caution. Winter nights can be particularly harsh, with freezing temperatures and icy roads. Also, reduced visibility adds to the difficulty of the job.

Night deliveries necessitate a keen sense of direction and familiarity with the route. Landmarks that are easily visible during the day may become obscured in the dark, making it more challenging. Additionally, the cold can be physically taxing, requiring drivers to wear layers of clothing that can hinder movement and make the job more strenuous. Despite these challenges, the commitment to ensuring that every package is delivered on time remains unwavering.

Safety is paramount during night deliveries, and slowing down is crucial. Darkness significantly reduces visibility, making it harder to see pedestrians, animals, or obstacles on the road. Slowing down allows drivers more time to react to unexpected situations, reducing the risk of accidents.

Caution extends beyond driving speed. Handling packages in the dark requires extra care to prevent trips and falls. Drivers must use adequate lighting, such as headlamps or flashlights, to ensure they can see their surroundings clearly. This not only helps in delivering packages safely but also in maintaining personal safety.

In winter, ice and snow can make roads slippery, requiring slower driving speeds and careful maneuvering.

Misloaded Packages

Misloaded packages are a frequent source of frustration, and the impact is magnified during night deliveries. A misloaded package means that a parcel intended for an early stop is buried under others meant for later deliveries. This mistake forces the driver to stop and unload parts of the truck, wasting precious time and increasing the risk of delays.

The process of searching for a misloaded package in the dark adds to the frustration, particularly when working against the clock.

Drivers must communicate the issue of misloaded packages with the dispatch team to ensure such mistakes are minimized in the future.

Daily Driving Distances and the High Number of Stops

On average, I drove 160 to 180 miles a day, with over 90 stops. This pace demands both physical and mental endurance. Driving long distances requires constant vigilance, especially at night. Fatigue can set in, making it crucial for drivers to take regular breaks and stay hydrated. The repetitive nature of the job can also lead to monotony, which drivers must combat by staying focused and engaged.

The high number of stops adds another layer of complexity. Each stop requires precise coordination to ensure packages are delivered to the correct addresses. The physical act of getting in and out of the truck, carrying packages, and traveling on different terrains keeps drivers constantly on the move and demands good physical health and stamina.

Adapting to Challenges

For younger drivers entering the delivery profession, maintaining a steady pace and adapting to daily surprises is key to long-term success. The job is a marathon, not a sprint, and pacing oneself is crucial to avoid burnout. New drivers should focus on consistency rather than speed.

Daily surprises are a constant in this line of work, from unexpected traffic jams to sudden changes in the delivery schedule. New drivers should develop a routine but remain adaptable, ready to handle any curveballs that come their way. Embracing these challenges as learning opportunities will help build resilience and improve overall performance.

The Physical Toll

In addition to the physical exertion, drivers often find themselves covered in dirt and grime by the end of the day. Handling packages that have been through various environments, being on dusty rural roads, or working in industrial areas all contribute to the accumulation of dirt. It's a job where you can't be afraid to get your hands dirty.

Drivers need to take care of their physical health by stretching regularly, staying hydrated, and eating well. Investing in good footwear and ergonomic supports can also help mitigate some of the physical strains of the job. Regular exercise and strength training can build the stamina and resilience needed to handle the daily grind.

Handling Hazardous Materials

Handling hazardous materials, ranging from chemicals to biological substances, is another critical aspect of the job that requires specialized knowledge and extreme caution. Drivers must be trained to identify hazardous packages, understand the potential dangers, and follow strict protocols for safe handling and delivery.

Proper protective equipment, such as gloves and safety goggles, is essential when handling hazardous materials. You must also be aware of emergency procedures in case of spills or exposure. The safe transportation of these materials is not just about complying with regulations but also about ensuring personal safety and the safety of others.

Personal Anecdotes of Hazardous Material Incidents

Over the years, I've had my share of hazardous material incidents that taught me valuable lessons about safety and preparedness. One of the most memorable occurred early in my career when a package containing stone acid leaked into the back of my truck.

Unaware of the leak, I continued my deliveries until I started to feel a burning sensation in my eyes. Realizing the danger, I immediately pulled over, got my water jug, and washed my eyes out.

Another harrowing experience involved a package of women's perm kits that broke open on a particularly hot summer day. The temperature in the back of the truck soared to over 140 degrees, and the chemicals in the kits reacted to the heat, releasing fumes that nearly overwhelmed me. I had to carefully ventilate the truck and ensure that the remaining packages were safe to handle.

Despite the routine nature of the job, there is always an element of unpredictability that requires constant vigilance and readiness to respond.

The Relief of Finishing the Day and Going Home

At the end of a long, demanding day, the relief of finishing the day and heading home is a welcome respite. After countless hours on the road, numerous stops, and handling all sorts of packages, the thought of returning home brings a sense of accomplishment and peace. The physical and mental exhaustion fades as we park the truck, complete the final check-ins, and clock out for the day.

This moment marks the transition from the high-paced, demanding environment of the delivery route to the comfort and familiarity of home. The knowledge that all packages have been delivered and the day's work is complete brings a deep sense of relief and satisfaction.

The Need for Decompression Time

After the hustle and bustle of the day, decompression time becomes essential. The high-intensity nature of the job can be overwhelming at times. So, taking time to unwind and decompress is crucial for mental and physical well-being.

Drivers often develop personal routines to help them transition from work mode to relaxation. This might include a quiet moment alone, engaging in a hobby, spending time with family, or simply enjoying a good meal. Decompression activities help to release the tension built up during the day and allow the body and mind to relax.

For me, I used to tell my wife to give me ten minutes to decompress after I got home. This short period allowed me to shift gears, let go of the day's stresses, and fully relax. Whether it's a brief walk, a quick nap, or simply sitting quietly, finding what works best is key to effective decompression.

Monitoring and Surveillance

In the modern era of delivery services, increased monitoring and tracking by the office have become standard practice. Advanced technology allows dispatchers to closely monitor every driver's movements, routes, and delivery times in real-time. GPS tracking systems provide detailed data on a driver's location, speed, and even driving habits.

While this technology can enhance efficiency and help optimize routes, it also adds a layer of pressure on drivers. Knowing that their every move is being tracked can be stressful, leading to a heightened sense of scrutiny and accountability. Drivers must balance the demands of the job with the awareness that any deviation from the planned route or delay can be instantly flagged and questioned by the office.

In addition to standard tracking, drivers occasionally face undercover surveillance. This can involve unknown individuals observing their work, noting their performance, and reporting back to management. The knowledge that someone could be watching at any time can be unnerving and adds additional pressure.

Undercover surveillance impacts drivers by creating a constant sense of being evaluated, which can affect their performance and morale. The fear of making a mistake while being watched can lead to increased anxiety and stress. However, it also encourages adherence to company policies and procedures, ensuring that drivers maintain high professionalism and safety standards.

The cumulative effect of a week's worth of deliveries, combined with the stress of constant monitoring and surveillance, leads to significant physical and mental exhaustion by the end of the week. Drivers often start their week with energy and optimism, but the relentless pace, long hours, and physical demands quickly take their toll. By Friday, even the most seasoned drivers feel the weight of the week's work.

Personal Rituals and Songs to Cope with the Stress

To cope with the stress and maintain their sanity, many drivers develop personal rituals and find solace in simple pleasures. These coping mechanisms are crucial for managing the day-to-day pressures and ensuring they remain motivated and focused.

One common ritual is listening to music. Many drivers have favorite songs or playlists that help them relax and stay upbeat. For instance, I used to sing on the belt on Fridays, "The eagle flies on Friday, Saturday I go out to play." This simple act of singing a familiar tune helped lighten the mood and was a reminder that the weekend was just around the corner.

Other drivers might engage in brief moments of mindfulness or meditation during breaks, helping to clear their minds and reduce stress. Some might enjoy a particular snack or beverage that gives them a small boost of comfort during their route. These small rituals, tailored to individual preferences, provide a much-needed mental break and help maintain a positive outlook.

Career Progression and Personal Life

For new delivery drivers, the journey often begins by covering vacations and handling temporary assignments. This period is a crucial stepping stone toward securing a permanent route and progressing to top pay. During these initial years, drivers must prove their reliability, adaptability, and competence. By successfully managing varied and often challenging assignments, they demonstrate their readiness for a full-time position.

The progression to top pay usually takes about four years, during which drivers gradually climb the pay scale. Each milestone achieved reflects their growing experience and dedication to the job. Reaching top pay is a significant accomplishment, offering financial stability and recognizing the driver's hard work and commitment.

Brown's Encouragement for Drivers to Settle Down and Buy Homes

Brown encourages its drivers to settle down and invest in their future. The stability and benefits associated with a long-term career in delivery provide an ideal foundation for building a life and purchasing a home. This encouragement stems from the company's recognition of the importance of a stable personal life in developing a dedicated and motivated workforce.

Owning a home brings a sense of security and achievement, which can positively impact a driver's overall well-being. The financial stability offered by a steady job and competitive pay allows drivers to make significant life investments, contributing to their sense of fulfillment and stability.

The High Divorce Rate Among Drivers and the Stress on Personal Relationships

Despite the benefits, the demanding nature of the job can take a toll on personal relationships. The high divorce rate among drivers shows the job's impact on family life. Long hours, unpredictable schedules, and the physical and mental exhaustion that come with the job can strain relationships to the breaking point.

The constant stress and the inability to predict when they will return home can create a sense of instability and isolation for both drivers and their families. The pressures of the job often leave little time or energy for nurturing personal relationships, leading to feelings of neglect and resentment.

The high divorce rate among delivery drivers is a sobering reality that reflects the significant stress and demands of the job. Long hours, unpredictable schedules, and the physical and mental exhaustion from the job can strain personal relationships to the breaking point. The constant pressure to meet delivery deadlines often leaves little time and energy for family life, leading to feelings of neglect and isolation for both drivers and their spouses.

Reflecting on my own experiences and those of my colleagues, I have seen firsthand how the demands of the job can impact marriages. Many drivers struggle to balance the intense workload with their responsibilities at home, and the resulting stress can lead to conflict and separation. The nature of the job often means missing out on important family events, further exacerbating the strain on relationships.

Despite these challenges, some drivers find ways to maintain strong family bonds. Open communication, mutual understanding, and finding time for family amidst a hectic schedule are crucial. However, the industry must also recognize these challenges and provide support to help drivers balance their professional and personal lives more effectively.

Choosing the Career for Life and the Benefits of Pension After 25-30 Years

For those who choose to stick with the career for life, the rewards are substantial. After 25 to 30 years of dedicated service, drivers become eligible for a pension that can significantly ease their financial burdens in retirement. This pension provides a steady income stream, allowing for a more comfortable and secure retirement.

Choosing this career for life means embracing both its challenges and its rewards. The benefits of a pension, coupled with the sense of achievement from a long and successful career, offer drivers a fulfilling and stable future. Despite the demanding nature of the job, many find that the financial security and the personal satisfaction derived from serving their communities make it all worthwhile.

Customer Relationships and Respect

One of the most rewarding aspects is the opportunity to build long-term relationships with customers. Treating customers with respect is the foundation of these relationships. We often become a familiar and trusted presence in the communities we serve, known not just for delivering packages but also for our reliability, courtesy, and professionalism.

Respecting customers means more than just timely deliveries. It involves understanding their needs, being courteous and polite, and going the extra mile to ensure their satisfaction. Whether it's helping an elderly customer carry a heavy package or waiting for someone to answer the door, these small acts of kindness and consideration go a long way in building strong, positive relationships.

Over the years, I have had numerous memorable interactions with customers that highlight the mutual respect and trust that can develop between a driver and the community. One such instance involved a customer who had been receiving packages from me for nearly two decades. This elderly gentleman would always wait at his door with a warm smile and a kind word. One winter, during a particularly harsh storm, I made sure his essential medications were delivered on time despite the challenging conditions. His heartfelt gratitude and the tears in his eyes reinforced the importance of our role in people's lives.

Another memorable experience was with a young mother who had just moved to the area. She was struggling to manage her toddler and handle her deliveries. Seeing her plight, I started placing her packages closer to her door to make it easier for her. Over time, this small gesture turned into a friendly rapport, and she often expressed her appreciation for the extra effort.

The Importance of Being a "Smooth Operator" Behind the Wheel

Being a "smooth operator" behind the wheel is crucial. This term goes beyond driving skills; it encompasses the ability to drive on the routes efficiently, handle the vehicle with care, and maintain composure under pressure. A smooth operator ensures that packages are delivered safely without delays or incidents.

Smooth driving involves anticipating and responding to traffic conditions, planning the best routes, and making quick, safe decisions on the road. It also means handling packages with care to prevent damage and ensuring that every delivery is made with the highest level of professionalism. Customers appreciate a driver who consistently demonstrates skill and reliability, reinforcing their trust in the service.

The Role of Seniority in Route Assignments

Seniority plays a significant role in route assignments within delivery companies. Drivers with more years of service often have the privilege of choosing preferred routes, which can lead to more predictable schedules and established customer relationships. This system rewards experience and loyalty, providing long-term drivers with a sense of stability and control over their work environment.

Seniority allows drivers to build a deep familiarity with their routes, which in turn enhances efficiency and customer service. Knowing the intricacies of a particular area, from the best parking spots to the specific needs of regular customers, enables senior drivers to perform their duties with exceptional proficiency.

For newer drivers, understanding the importance of seniority is essential. It provides a clear incentive to stay with the company and work toward earning these benefits. Senior drivers often serve as mentors, sharing their knowledge and experience to help newer drivers succeed and eventually earn their own preferred routes.

The Uniqueness of Being on the Same Route for 29 Years

Spending 29 years on the same delivery route is a rarity in any profession, but it has provided me with a unique perspective on the job. Over these three decades, I have witnessed the ebb and flow of communities, the growth of families, and the changing landscape of my delivery area. This long-term consistency allowed me to build deep relationships with my customers, who came to see me as a reliable and familiar presence in their daily lives.

Staying on the same route for such an extended period developed a sense of stability and continuity that benefitted my customers and me. I learned the most efficient ways, the best times to avoid traffic, and the specific preferences of my regular recipients. This intimate knowledge helped me perform my job with exceptional efficiency and personalized service, earning the trust and respect of the community I served.

The Respect and Challenges Associated with Being a Brown Driver

Being a Brown driver comes with a unique set of challenges and opportunities to earn respect. The uniform and the truck are symbols of reliability and professionalism, and living up to these expectations is a daily commitment.

The respect associated with being a Brown driver is earned through consistent performance, courteous interactions, and a steadfast commitment to service.

Customers appreciate drivers who go above and beyond; this respect is reciprocated through loyalty and trust. However, the challenges are significant: long hours, physical strain, and the need to maintain a high level of focus and professionalism. Overcoming these challenges and maintaining a positive attitude are crucial for success in this role.

The Impact of My Military Background on Customer Interactions

My military background significantly influenced my approach to the job and my interactions with customers. The discipline, punctuality, and attention to detail ingrained in me during my military service translated seamlessly into my work as a delivery driver. Customers often noticed and appreciated my punctuality, reliability, and the neatness with which I handled their deliveries.

Military service also instilled a strong sense of respect and courtesy, which I carried into my civilian career. Addressing customers with politeness and maintaining a respectful demeanor helped build strong relationships. My background also made me more resilient and adaptable, enabling me to handle the physical and mental demands of the job effectively.

One of my customers, a veteran himself, once told me how much he appreciated my disciplined approach and the care I took with his deliveries. Our shared military background created a bond of mutual respect, reinforcing the importance of professionalism and reliability in my work.

Various Roles Taken on for Customers

Throughout my career, I found myself taking on a variety of roles beyond simply delivering packages. These roles emerged naturally from daily interactions with customers and the relationships built over time. My primary responsibility was to ensure that packages were delivered on time and in good condition. However, the job often required more than just dropping off a package. I became a **confidant** for many customers who would share their personal stories and struggles during our brief interactions. Listening to their concerns and offering a sympathetic ear became a valued part of my service.

In some instances, I found myself offering to help elderly or physically limited customers with heavy packages. My willingness to assist with lifting and carrying items inside their homes or businesses was greatly appreciated and helped build trust and rapport.

Similarly, I often assumed the role of an amateur **psychologist**, offering words of encouragement and support to customers going through tough times. Whether it was a few kind words or a simple gesture of understanding, these small acts of kindness made a significant difference in their lives.

My preacher role emerged from my faith and willingness to share uplifting messages with customers who needed spiritual support. Conversations about faith and hope became a source of comfort for many, creating deeper connections beyond the usual delivery interactions.

Finally, many customers came to see me as a **friend**. Over the years, I developed strong bonds with numerous individuals, celebrating their joys and supporting them through hardships. These friendships enriched my work experience and added a personal touch to my daily routine.

The bonds formed with customers over the years did not end with my retirement. Many of the people I served continued to inquire about me, asking my successor about my well-being and expressing their gratitude for the years of dedicated service.

One particularly heartwarming example is a customer who had been receiving packages from me for over two decades. Even after I retired, she would often ask the new driver about me, sharing fond memories of our interactions and expressing her hope that I was enjoying my retirement.

Another customer, whom I helped regularly with heavy packages, sent me a thank-you note after learning about my retirement, expressing how much my assistance had meant to her.

These continued inquiries and expressions of gratitude show the lasting impact that delivery drivers can have on the community they serve. The relationships built through years of consistent, caring service create a legacy of trust and respect that endures long after the deliveries have ended.

Working as a delivery driver is a profession that embodies a love-and-hate relationship. On one hand, the job offers a sense of freedom, the satisfaction of physical activity, and the joy of serving the community. On the other hand, it presents significant challenges, including long hours, physical exhaustion, and constant pressure to meet deadlines. This duality is what makes the job both rewarding and demanding. The love comes from the connections made, the trust built with customers, and the sense of accomplishment from overcoming daily obstacles. The hate arises from the relentless pace, the physical toll on the body, and the stress of facing traffic and tight schedules.

The career has left a lasting mark on my personal and professional life, teaching invaluable lessons and forging meaningful connections that endure long after the last package is delivered.

CHAPTER 12
Angel on My Shoulder

In every career, there are moments that stand out as particularly challenging or memorable. For me, the worst day in my career at Brown happened during my second year of driving. It was a day that started like any other, but it ended up being a test of my determination.

The Incident

It was early morning, and the sun had just begun to peek over the horizon. I was on my usual route, delivering packages with the precision and reliability that my customers had come to expect. The air was crisp, and the hum of the engine was a familiar comfort as I moved through the city streets. Little did I know that this routine day would soon take a drastic turn.

On that fateful day, as I parked at the bustling loading dock, I prepared to make my delivery. The dock was bustling with activities—forklifts whizzing by, workers unloading goods, and the constant clatter of machinery.

As I finished unloading, I jumped off the dock. My rear door did not go all the way up. The truck door was a formidable piece of equipment, weighing in at a hefty 280 pounds. It was designed to be sturdy and secure, featuring a four-inch pointed union latch that locked the door in place. This latch, while essential for keeping the door shut during transit, was a hazard if mishandled. Its pointed end was sharp and unforgiving, a detail that I had always been cautious about.

So, before I could react, the four-inch pointed latch embedded itself into my skull. The pain was instantaneous and excruciating, a searing shock that radiated through my head.

I had experienced pain before. Playing organized football for eight years taught me a lot about physical endurance. I had taken hits on the field that left me dazed and bruised. My time in the army, playing combat football, pushed my body to its limits with the sheer intensity of the physical confrontations. Even working as a bouncer in a rowdy Austin Texas saloon, where I dealt with bar fights and unruly patrons, had toughened me up. But none of these experiences compared to the agony I felt at that moment.

This was different. The union latch had pierced my skin and bone, sending shockwaves of pain through my entire body. Blood gushed from the wound, flowing down my face and soaking my clothes. I was momentarily paralyzed by the intensity of it, unable to comprehend the full extent of my injury.

The sight of my own blood pouring out was concerning. I looked like Rick Flair after a sixty-minute match. I had been through rough situations before, but this was on another level. The union latch had delivered a blow that I had never anticipated, marking a pivotal and harrowing point in my career.

Immediate Aftermath

As the shock of the injury set in, my first instinct was to call the office. This was before the era of cell phones, so I had to rely on a landline. I went towards the office phone, blood streaming down my face and blurring my vision. I dialed the number with trembling hands, but there was no answer. The line rang and rang, the silence on the other end only adding to my growing sense of concern.

By this time, the customers at the loading dock had noticed my distress. Their initial confusion quickly turned to alarm as they saw the extent of my injury. Blood was pooling on the ground, and my clothes were soaked. Several of them rushed over, their faces etched with concern. One of them, an older gentleman, immediately suggested calling an ambulance.

"You need medical help right away," he insisted.

But I was determined to get the truck back to the terminal. Despite the pain and the blood loss, my mind was fixed on my responsibilities. I still had twenty more deliveries to make, and I couldn't let my customers down. The thought of leaving the packages undelivered and the truck unattended was unacceptable to me.

"No," I said, my voice strained but resolute. "I have to get back to the terminal."

Seeing my determination, the customers quickly rallied around to help. One of them handed me a towel to press against the wound. I pressed it to my head, feeling the warm blood soak into the fabric. The pain was intense, but I knew I had to keep going. Others began cleaning up the blood that had spilled onto the floor, their actions swift and efficient.

Their concern and quick thinking provided a lifeline in that chaotic moment.

The Journey to the Terminal

Driving back to the terminal was one of the most challenging tasks I had ever faced. With the towel pressed firmly against my head, I started the engine and began the drive back to the terminal. Every jolt and bump in the road sent fresh waves of pain through my skull, but I kept my focus on the task at hand. Changing a five-speed and holding a rag on one's head was a daunting task.

As I moved through the streets, I could feel the blood continuing to flow. My vision was blurred by the constant flow of blood, and I had to blink rapidly to keep my eyes clear.

My head throbbed with each heartbeat. Yet, the support of the customers gave me the strength to push through. They had shown me kindness and concern when I needed it most, and that gave me the resolve to keep going.

The towel was quickly becoming saturated, but I pressed on, knowing I had to get back to the terminal, not just for the sake of the deliveries but also to find someone who could take over and ensure the packages reached their destinations. My determination to fulfill my duties, combined with the assistance from those around me, helped me overcome the immediate aftermath of the accident.

The drive felt interminable. Time seemed to stretch, and each mile seemed to be a test of my endurance. I could feel my strength waning, but my determination kept me going. The responsibility I felt for my job and my customers was a powerful motivator, pushing me to keep moving forward despite the pain.

At the Terminal

Finally, the terminal came into view. Relief washed over me as I pulled into the parking lot, but the struggle was far from over. I parked the truck and got out, still holding the towel to my head. Blood was still trickling down my face, and I knew I needed immediate medical attention.

As I made my way toward the office, I encountered Laura Brown, a customer service rep who, by chance, had stopped by the terminal. The moment she saw me, her eyes widened in shock. Without hesitation, she rushed over to me.

"Oh, my God, what happened?" she exclaimed, her voice filled with concern.

I tried to explain, but this time, I was in a compromising position. Laura took one look at my condition and made an immediate decision.

"We need to get you to the emergency room right now," she said firmly.

I didn't have the strength to argue. I could feel myself slipping into a more vulnerable state, and I knew she was right. Laura told me into her car, her actions swift and decisive. As she drove, I could see the worry etched on her face, but her calm demeanor was a source of comfort.

In the Emergency Room

The ride to the emergency room was a blur. The pain and blood loss were taking their toll. Laura's presence was a lifeline; her determination to get me the help I needed showed her true character.

When we finally arrived at the emergency room, Laura rushed inside to get medical staff. I was quickly taken in and given the treatment I needed.

In the emergency room, the medical staff quickly took over, assessing the severity of my injury. I was wheeled into a treatment room, and a flurry of activity surrounded me as nurses and doctors worked to stop the bleeding and clean the wound.

The doctor, a calm and focused professional, examined the gash on my head. He explained that I would need stitches to close the wound and prevent further blood loss. As he worked, I felt a mixture of pain and relief. Each stitch tugged at my skin meant that I was on the path to recovery.

Nineteen stitches later, the wound was finally closed. The pain had dulled to a throbbing ache, and I was beginning to feel more like myself again.

As the doctors stitched up my wound, I couldn't help but feel immense gratitude for Laura. Her quick thinking and decisive action had made all the difference, and I knew I owed her a debt of gratitude.

The doctor gave me instructions for care and advised me to take it easy for a few days. However, knowing my responsibilities and the work that still needed to be done, I couldn't imagine taking time off.

Laura Brown stayed with me throughout the entire process, and her presence was a comforting constant. Once the medical team was satisfied with my condition. We drove back to the terminal, and the journey was much quieter than before. I was exhausted, both physically and mentally, but grateful for Laura's unwavering support.

Back to Terminal

When we arrived at the terminal, it was eerily quiet. The usual hustle and bustle of the place were absent, and there was no sign of the manager. We looked around, hoping to find someone in charge, but the office was empty.

The absence of a manager was perplexing and frustrating. I needed to report the incident and ensure that someone could take over my deliveries. I felt a sense of duty to inform my colleagues about what had happened and to ensure that the packages I had been carrying would reach their destinations.

Laura and I waited for a while, hoping that the manager would return. During this time, she continued to express her concern for my well-being, making sure I was comfortable and had everything I needed. Her dedication and kindness were overwhelming, and I knew that without her, the situation could have been much worse.

Despite the challenges of the day and the absence of a manager, I felt a sense of accomplishment. I had managed to get the necessary medical treatment, thanks to Laura's quick thinking, and I had taken steps to ensure that my responsibilities were communicated effectively. It was a day that tested my limits, but it also revealed the incredible support and resilience within the team.

Back on the Road

After the chaos of the day, most people would have taken the doctor's advice to rest and recover. However, I couldn't shake the sense of duty I felt toward my customers and the commitments I had made. Despite the stitches and the exhaustion, I made the decision to return to the road to complete my pickup run.

My customers had come to rely on my punctuality and reliability. They often told me they could set their watches by my arrivals and departures. I had built strong relationships with them over the years, and I knew that many of them would be wondering what had happened to me. They counted on me not just for their deliveries but as a dependable part of their routine.

As I prepared to head back out, Laura Brown watched me with concern. She had seen the extent of my injury and knew the physical strain I was under. "You've been through a lot today. Let someone else handle it."

I appreciated her concern, but my sense of responsibility was stronger. "I'll be fine," I reassured her, even though I wasn't entirely sure myself. "I need to get back out there. My customers are expecting me."

Laura wasn't convinced. "At least let me come with you," she said, determined to ensure I didn't push myself too hard. Her offer was kind, and I knew it came from a place of genuine care, but I felt that I needed to handle this on my own. It was part of my job, and I didn't want to burden her further after everything she had already done for me.

"No," I said gently but firmly. "I can manage. You've already done so much. Thank you, Laura, but I need to do this myself."

Reluctantly, she nodded, understanding my need to fulfill my duty. As I drove off, I could see the worry in her eyes, but I also saw a hint of admiration. She knew that sometimes, the drive to meet our commitments could be stronger than the pain we endure.

Returning to the route, I was greeted by familiar faces, their concern evident as they saw the bandage on my head. "What happened to you?" one of them asked, eyes wide with shock.

"It's a long story," I replied with a weary smile. "But I'm here to finish what I started."

Their reactions varied from disbelief to admiration. They offered words of encouragement and gratitude, their appreciation for my dedication clear. Despite the pain and exhaustion, seeing their relief and knowing that I was making a difference kept me going.

The drive was grueling, and each moment was a test of my endurance. But with every package I delivered, I felt a sense of accomplishment. I had faced one of the toughest challenges in my career and came out on the other side stronger and more determined.

By the end of the day, I was completely spent. The physical toll was immense, but the sense of duty fulfilled made it all worthwhile.

Completing the route was an ordeal, but the sense of duty and responsibility kept me moving forward. When I finally returned to the terminal, the sun was setting, casting a warm glow over the familiar surroundings.

As I parked the truck and stepped out, I was greeted by a few of the older drivers who had already finished their routes. Their reactions to seeing me were a mix of surprise and admiration. They had heard about the accident, but seeing the bandages and the weariness in my eyes made it real for them.

"You should not have gone back on the road," one of the older drivers, Jim, remarked, shaking his head in disbelief. "I can't believe you finished your route after all that."

"Had to," I replied with a tired smile. "Customers were counting on me."

They nodded, understanding the sense of duty that comes with the job. Their respect and support were evident, and it bolstered my spirits, reminding me that I wasn't alone in this. But looking back, it was not too smart finishing the route.

The Accident Report

Next, I had to fill out the accident report. It was a necessary part of the process, ensuring that everything was documented accurately.

I sat down at the desk, the paperwork spread out in front of me, and began to write. From the moment the latch struck to the drive back to the terminal, each detail had to be recorded.

As I wrote, more drivers began to gather around. Word had spread quickly about the incident, and curiosity drew them in. They wanted to see the injury that had everyone talking. Each time someone new walked in, I could see the shock on their faces as they took in the bandages and the weary expression on my face.

"Let me see that head of yours," one of them said, leaning in for a closer look. "That's one nasty gash."

"Yeah," I replied, lifting the edge of the bandage slightly to show the stitches. "Nineteen stitches. Not exactly how I planned to spend my day."

They winced in sympathy, each offering their own version of support. Knowing that my actions had garnered such respect from my peers was a humbling experience.

As I finished the accident report, the sense of finality began to set in. The day's events had been challenging, but I had made it through with the support of my colleagues and the determination to see it through. The drivers who had gathered around me began to disperse, each offering a pat on the back or a word of encouragement as they left.

The terminal was starting to quiet down as the day's work was coming to an end. I looked around, taking in the familiar sights and sounds, feeling a deep sense of gratitude for the support I had received. It had been a tough day, but it had also been a reminder of the strength of the community and the power of determination.

As I left the terminal that evening, I knew that the experience had changed me. It had tested my limits and shown me the depth of my own resilience. And it reinforced the bonds I shared with my fellow drivers, who stood by me through one of the most challenging days of my career.

Follow-up with Supervisors

Five months after the incident, just as the memory of that harrowing day was beginning to fade, an unusual event took place. I was assigned a ride-along with not just one but two supervisors. Laura, the customer service rep who had helped me get to the emergency room, and another supervisor I had never met before. The presence of two supervisors was highly unusual and immediately set my nerves on edge.

The day began like any other. I arrived at the terminal early, ready to start my route. Laura and the unknown supervisor were already waiting for me, their expressions serious and focused. Laura greeted me with a warm, albeit professional, smile while the other supervisor remained silent, observing me closely.

"Good morning," Laura said, her tone conveying both familiarity and authority. "We'll be riding along with you today."

I nodded, masking my surprise. "Sure thing," I replied, trying to keep my tone casual. "Let's get started."

We climbed into the truck, and I took my usual spot behind the wheel. Laura sat beside me while the other supervisor positioned himself in the back, a clipboard in hand.

As I started the engine and pulled out of the terminal, the weight of their presence was intense. Having one supervisor ride along was standard practice. But riding with two was unheard of.

The first few hours were tense. Laura occasionally asked questions about my route and my customers, her demeanor supportive yet inquisitive. The other supervisor remained silent, scribbling notes on his clipboard. The atmosphere in the truck was heavy with unspoken questions, and I couldn't shake the feeling that I was being closely scrutinized.

About halfway through the day, as we passed through a particularly busy area, Laura turned to the other supervisor. "Have you seen what you needed to see?" she asked, her tone calm but pointed.

He looked up from his clipboard, meeting her gaze with a nod. "Yes, I have," he replied simply, his expression neutral.

The rest of the ride continued in a similar fashion. I focused on my driving and deliveries, maintaining my usual level of professionalism despite the scrutiny. Laura and the other supervisor continued their observations, but the tension began to ease slightly after their brief exchange.

As the six-hour ride-along drew to a close, we returned to the terminal. Laura and the other supervisor thanked me for my time and professionalism, and their tones are more relaxed now. I couldn't help but feel a sense of relief as I parked the truck and prepared to end the day.

Before they left, Laura pulled me aside. "You did well today," she said, her smile genuine. "We just needed to ensure that everything was running smoothly after the incident. Upper management wanted to make sure there were no lingering issues."

I nodded, understanding the reasoning behind the ride-along. "I appreciate the feedback," I replied. "I'm just doing my job."

She patted my shoulder reassuringly. "And you're doing it well. Keep up the good work."

As Laura and the other supervisor walked away, I reflected on the day's events. The unusual nature of the double ride-along had been nerve-wracking, but it had also provided an opportunity to demonstrate my dedication to my job. Their observations and feedback affirmed that I was on the right track, reinforcing my commitment to my job and my customers.

In the days that followed, the ride-along became a topic of conversation among my colleagues. They were curious about the unusual setup and the reasons behind it. I shared my experience, emphasizing the importance of staying professional and focused, no matter the circumstances.

Ultimately, the follow-up with the supervisors served as a reminder of the challenges and expectations that come with the job. It reinforced the importance of dedication and professionalism— qualities that had seen me through the toughest days and would continue to guide me in the future.

As time passed, the memory of that challenging day at the loading dock began to fade, but the impact it had on me remained strong. I never saw Laura again after the follow-up ride-along. Her role seemed to be a temporary assignment, or perhaps she moved on to another position within the company. However, the help she provided during one of the most difficult moments of my career left a lasting impression.

I often found myself reflecting on her quick thinking and decisive actions that day. Without her intervention, the outcome could have been much worse. Although our paths never crossed again, I will always remember her as the angel on my shoulder, guiding me through that critical moment.

One day, as I was finishing up my shift, a driver supervisor approached me. "You know, the upper management thought the head wound had done something to you," he said almost casually.

I raised an eyebrow, intrigued and slightly amused.

"They thought maybe the head wound had done something to you," he continued, shaking his head. "Can you imagine that?"

I couldn't help but chuckle at the absurdity of the notion. "Imagine that," I replied, my tone light. "I guess they have to cover all their bases."

We both laughed, and the conversation turned to other topics. But that comment stayed with me.

My thoughts often drifted back to the incident and the aftermath. The image of Laura's car, smeared with my blood, lingered in my mind. I felt a deep sense of gratitude for her help but also a pang of guilt for the mess I had made in her vehicle. It was a small price to pay for the assistance she provided, but it bothered me nonetheless.

In the grand scheme of things, the bloodstains were a minor inconvenience compared to the help she had given me. But it was a reflection of the deep gratitude I felt for her actions.

Reflecting on the incident, I realized it had taught me several valuable lessons. It reinforced the importance of determination. Despite the pain and the challenges, I pushed through and fulfilled my responsibilities. It also highlighted the strength of community and support, both from my colleagues and the customers who had helped me in my time of need.

The incident also served as a reminder of the complexities of working within a large organization. Upper management's suspicions, while misguided, were a part of the checks and balances that come with the territory. It emphasized the need for clear communication and understanding between different levels of the company.

Laura's actions and the support of my colleagues made all the difference. That day reinforced my commitment to my job and my community. As I continue my journey, I carry these lessons with me. The gratitude I feel for those who helped me, the reflection on the challenges I faced, and the commitment to always do my best. It's these experiences that shape us and remind us of the strength we possess.

And as I used to tell management, that it's my blood and my sweat.

CHAPTER 13
My Last Accident Witnessed

Every day on the road is different. You never truly know what you will encounter around the next bend or over the next hill. The unpredictability of each journey keeps you on your toes, ready for anything that might come your way. Whether it's moving through unexpected weather changes, dealing with road construction, or encountering wildlife, each day brings its own set of challenges and surprises.

This chapter echoes the sentiment I shared earlier in "You Never Know What You Will See." In that chapter, I recounted many unexpected situations that arise while on the road. From random acts of kindness to sudden emergencies, each day shows that the road holds many mysteries and experiences waiting to unfold.

Reflecting on these experiences, it's clear that being a delivery driver is about more than just transporting goods from point A to point B. It's about being prepared for the unexpected, staying alert, and being ready to assist others in times of need. The incident I'll share in this chapter illustrates how an ordinary day can quickly turn extraordinary and demand immediate, decisive action.

In this particular instance, what started as a routine delivery route transformed into a life-or-death situation in a matter of seconds. The sight of an orange Harley speeding past, followed by a sudden, catastrophic accident, shows the reality that you can never fully predict what lies ahead. It reinforces the idea that skills and vigilance cultivated on the road are crucial, not just for personal safety but for potentially saving lives.

So, it was a clear, sunny day as I set out on my delivery route, heading outside of Love Valley. The road ahead was a familiar one, winding through the scenic countryside with gentle hills and sweeping curves.

As I began my ascent up one of the larger hills, I couldn't help but appreciate the tranquility of the surroundings. The peacefulness of the day, however, was about to be shattered by a sudden and alarming event.

As I climbed the hill, I noticed an orange Harley-Davidson motorcycle approaching from the opposite direction, coming down the hill at a considerable speed.

The bright color of the bike caught my eye, standing out vividly against the backdrop of the green fields. As the rider came closer, something else grabbed my attention—his hands. They were vibrating noticeably on the handlebars, a clear sign of instability or an issue with the bike.

Instinctively, I kept my eye on the rider in my mirror as he passed by. There was something unsettling about the way his hands shook, and I couldn't shake the feeling that something was wrong. My concern quickly turned to horror as, just as the rider reached the bottom of the hill, I saw him shoot straight up off the motorcycle. The sight was surreal as if time slowed down for a moment.

The rider was launched into the air, and for a split second, he seemed suspended above the bike. Then, gravity took over, and he came crashing down, landing violently in the middle of the road. His motorcycle continued its uncontrolled journey, skidding and tumbling until it came to rest several feet away from where he had fallen.

Without a second thought, I turned my vehicle around and rushed to the scene. My heart pounded as I approached, the magnitude of the situation becoming clearer with each passing second. The once peaceful road was now a scene of chaos, with the rider lying motionless in the middle of it. The quiet countryside was disrupted by the reality of a life-threatening accident.

Upon reaching him, I saw a young man, no older than his early thirties, struggling for his life. His body was contorted in an unnatural position, and he appeared to be barely conscious. The gravity of the situation hit me hard, but there was no time to hesitate. I needed to act quickly to get him the help he desperately needed.

The calm of the countryside had been replaced by a sense of urgency and adrenaline. As I pulled up next to the fallen rider, I could see the severity of his injuries more clearly.

As I stood over the injured rider, the severity of his condition became increasingly evident. He was lying on his side, his body contorted awkwardly from the impact. His breathing was labored and accompanied by a gurgling sound, indicating fluid in his airway or lungs. His half-open eyes were glassy and unfocused.

It was clear that something was terribly wrong beyond the visible injuries. His chest rose and fell irregularly, and his skin had a pallid, almost grayish hue, suggesting that his oxygen levels were dangerously low.

The gurgling noise was a sign that his airway was partially obstructed, possibly by blood or other bodily fluids. His limbs were unnaturally twisted. Despite these severe injuries, he was still conscious, though barely.

My first instinct was to call for help, but I remembered that this area often had poor service. I dialed 911. To my immense relief, the call went through. I quickly explained the situation to the dispatcher, detailing the location of the accident and the condition of the rider. The dispatcher assured me that help was on the way and advised me to stay with the rider and keep him as still and calm as possible.

Despite the rural location, the response from the local fire station, just two miles away, was impressively rapid. Within minutes, I could hear the wail of sirens in the distance, growing louder as the emergency vehicles approached.

The first responders arrived quickly, their presence bringing a glimmer of hope. I recognized some of them as local neighbors, including one who worked part-time as a Brown preloader. Their familiarity with the area and the rider's likely identity added a personal touch to their urgency and care.

While waiting for the emergency responders, I made a second phone call, this time to my center manager. I knew it was important to inform him of the situation, as I would be delayed in completing my deliveries. I explained the accident and my involvement in assisting the injured rider and told him I was here for the duration.

My manager, understanding the gravity of the situation, assured me that I had done the right thing by stopping to help and told me to keep him updated as things progressed.

As the firefighters and paramedics took over, their training and professionalism were evident. They assessed the young man's injuries quickly, stabilizing him and preparing him for transport. The decision was made to take him to Winston Salem Baptist, our best hospital in North Carolina, instead of the closest local hospital. This choice, I later believed, played a crucial role in saving his life.

Throughout the ordeal, the young man's gurgling breaths and sporadic attempts to speak haunted me. It reminded me of the fact that how fragile life can be and how quickly things can change. The immediate response from the local emergency services and the support from my manager showed the importance of community and readiness to act in the face of unexpected emergencies.

Upon arrival at Winston Salem Baptist Hospital, the young rider was immediately rushed into the emergency room. The trauma team sprang into action, assessing his injuries and working to stabilize him. He was quickly diagnosed with a severe head injury, a fracture, and internal injuries that required urgent attention.

To immobilize his neck and spine and prevent further damage, the doctors placed him in a halo cast. This device, a rigid brace that encircles the head and is attached to the shoulders, was crucial for ensuring his spinal column remained stable. A band was secured around his head, adding additional support and protection to his fragile condition.

The family was called in multiple times and kept abreast of his condition and the critical procedures being performed. The uncertainty and gravity of his situation weighed heavily on everyone involved.

Word of the young rider's accident spread quickly through the community. Friends, neighbors, and even strangers who heard about his plight offered their support. The community rallied around the family, offering prayers and well-wishes for his recovery.

On a personal level, I found myself deeply affected by the incident. The image of the rider lying on the road, fighting for his life, was etched into my mind. Each day, I prayed for his recovery, hoping that the young man would pull through this ordeal. The collective power of these prayers and positive thoughts seemed to create a palpable sense of hope.

Against all odds, the young rider began to show signs of improvement. Slowly but surely, his condition stabilized, and he started the long journey toward recovery. The doctors and nurses were amazed at his resilience, noting that his recovery was nothing short of miraculous.

After spending numerous days in the halo cast, his condition improved enough for the device to be removed. The medical team then focused on his other injuries. He underwent months of intensive physical therapy and surgery, including a critical procedure on his shoulder. Each step was painstaking and required immense effort and determination on his part.

One of the most remarkable aspects of his recovery was his ability to resume driving his tractor-trailer. This milestone symbolized his return to a semblance of normalcy and independence. Despite the severity of his injuries, he was able to get back to doing what he loved.

However, the accident left a lasting impact on his eyesight. He often mentioned that his vision had changed significantly since the accident. The trauma had affected his eyes in a way that altered his perception and clarity. While this was a permanent change, he adapted and learned to live with the new reality.

As the young rider's health improved and he began to regain his strength, he felt a strong sense of gratitude and a need to acknowledge those who had helped him during his ordeal.

One of his first actions upon regaining his faculties was to call Brown's 1-800 number. He wanted to report the incident and ensure that the person who had assisted him received proper recognition.

The call connected him to one of Brown's contract employees, who listened intently as the rider recounted the details of the accident and the immediate aftermath.

The young man explained how he had been thrown from his motorcycle and how a passing driver had turned around, called for help, and stayed by his side until emergency services arrived. The gravity of his account was evident, and the employee promised to relay the information to the safety department.

Shortly after, Brown's safety department reached out to the rider to gather more information about the incident. They were particularly interested in understanding the actions taken by the driver who had assisted him. The rider emphasized the quick thinking and decisive actions that had likely saved his life, ensuring that the company understood the importance of the driver's intervention.

The injured rider's testimony was a heartfelt expression of gratitude. He detailed the events of that fateful day, highlighting the crucial moments when he was lying helpless in the middle of the road. He described how, amidst his pain and fear, the presence of the driver provided a lifeline, both literally and figuratively.

The rider articulated how the driver's actions—calling 911 despite the poor service area and staying with him until help arrived—were pivotal in his survival and recovery.

His testimony was more than just a recounting of events; it was a tribute to the driver's compassion and presence of mind. The rider made it clear that without the intervention of the driver, the outcome could have been drastically different.

The rider's heartfelt testimony and the subsequent report to Brown's safety department did not go unnoticed. Brown decided to publicly recognize the actions of the driver who had played such a crucial role in saving a life.

So, during the PCMI, I was called in front of the entire drivers' group.

Standing before my peers, I received a formal commendation. The company emphasized the importance of being prepared to act in emergencies and celebrated my response.

During the PCM, one of the fellow drivers spoke up, saying he would have done the same thing in a similar situation. The comment was a reassuring reminder that in the face of adversity, there is a shared sense of duty and compassion among the drivers. The supportive comment also reinforced the camaraderie and mutual respect within the group.

The recognition from Brown and the supportive response from my peers left a lasting impression on me. It was a moment of pride and affirmation that my actions were not only noticed but deeply appreciated. The incident and the acknowledgment that followed highlighted the profound impact that individuals can have on each other's lives, often in unexpected ways.

Reflecting on my years on the road, I realize just how rare it is to encounter a situation that demands immediate, life-saving intervention.

As a driver, I've seen my fair share of accidents and incidents, but most of them were minor or had already been attended to by the time I arrived. This particular incident, however, was different. It showed me how quickly a routine day can turn into a critical emergency. The immediacy of the young man's need for help and the severity of his condition I hadn't seen since my days as a soldier in Thailand and my days as a bouncer in saloons in Texas

In previous situations, I had been a bystander, watching from a distance or providing minimal assistance. But this time, I was thrust once again into the role of a first responder. The gravity of the moment, the urgency of the actions required, and the life-or-death stakes made this experience profoundly impactful. It was a humbling reminder of the unpredictability of life and the importance of being prepared to act when someone is in dire need.

The incident left a lasting personal impact on me. The memory of finding the young man, struggling for his life, is something that will stay with me forever.

As I approached him that day, I was struck by the eerie juxtaposition of the scene. Amidst the chaos, his motorcycle's stereo was still playing a country song, "Good God Almighty," which repeated the same line over and over. The surreal nature of that moment—the familiar melody playing as the backdrop to a life-and-death situation—etched itself into my mind. Well, he was there the whole time.

Name Tag on the Locker: At the terminal, my name tag remained on my locker, a shred of silent evidence of the years I had spent there and the experiences I had accumulated. It was more than just a marker of identity; it was a symbol of the dedication and commitment I had shown over the years.

Combination Given to a Younger Driver: When I decided to step back from my active role, I passed on the combination to my locker to a younger driver. This act symbolized the transfer of responsibility and the hope that the new generation would carry forward the values and lessons learned from such experiences.

Pal Label Stating "Hero": Perhaps the most touching and enduring acknowledgment was the Pal Label on my truck route. Pal Labels are typically used to designate which truck a package should go to, often numbered to simplify the route. My Pal Label, however, simply stated, "Hero." This small strip of white paper carried a profound message, encapsulating the essence of the actions taken during my career.

This incident was not just about the immediate response to a crisis. It was about the lasting effects of our actions, the legacy we leave behind, and the profound connections we forge through acts of compassion and courage.

The recognition and respect from my peers and the company reinforced the idea that sometimes, in the most unexpected moments, we are called upon to make a difference—and those moments can define us in ways we never imagined.

CHAPTER 14
My Observations

Having spent more than half of my life working at Brown, I have accumulated a wealth of experiences and insights that I believe are both valid and valuable.

My tenure at Brown, the largest shipping company in the world, has provided me with a unique perspective on its operations and evolution.

I have witnessed firsthand the company's growth, challenges, and technological advancements. This extensive experience forms the basis of my observations and reflections, which I will share in this chapter.

My journey with Brown has been long and eventful, and I feel confident that my observations will resonate with others who have been part of this remarkable organization.

When I started at Brown, the process of tracking packages was entirely manual. We had to write down every package's details with a six-digit tracking number. This labor-intensive process required meticulous attention to detail. Each stop, each mile, and each pickup piece had to be counted and recorded manually. The days were long, and the work was physically and mentally exhausting.

The manual process was not just about writing down numbers; it involved ensuring accuracy and reliability in every entry. This level of detail was crucial because any error could lead to lost packages and unhappy customers. Despite the challenges, there was a sense of pride in maintaining accurate records and ensuring that every package reached its destination.

As I look back on those early days, I remember the camaraderie among the drivers and the sense of accomplishment we felt when we completed our routes successfully. The work was tough, but it built character and a strong work ethic. We learned to rely on each other and to support one another through the daily grind. These experiences laid the foundation for my career and shaped my approach to work and life.

Technological Advancements

Over the years, Brown has embraced technology in ways that have revolutionized our work. The transition from manual tracking to digital systems marked a significant milestone. Now, instead of writing down tracking numbers, we simply take a picture of the package. This shift has streamlined the process, reduced errors, and increased efficiency.

The new technology has made our jobs easier and allowed us to handle more packages with greater accuracy. The handheld devices that once caused so much frustration have been replaced by advanced systems that automate many of the tasks we used to do manually. This transformation has improved productivity and enhanced the overall customer experience.

With these technological advancements came a period of adjustment. Many of us who had been with the company for years had to learn new skills and adapt to new ways of doing things. There were initial challenges, as with any significant change, but the benefits soon became apparent. The ability to track packages in real-time, provide customers with up-to-date information, and streamline operations has had a profound impact on the business.

These advancements also brought about a shift in the company culture. There was a renewed focus on innovation and continuous improvement. Training programs were implemented to ensure that all employees could make the most of the new technology. This investment in our development showed the company's commitment to staying at the forefront of the industry.

Personal Challenges

Throughout my career, I have faced numerous personal challenges. One of the most significant was my hand injury, which occurred before I joined Brown. I had cut off the tip of my ring finger and half of my thumb and crushed my right hand while working as a roughneck on an oil rig outside of La Grange, Texas. Despite this injury, I was determined to work and contribute.

My manager often told me that I needed to improve the neatness of my records. My response was always the same: "Remember when you hired me? I told you I was damaged goods. I showed you my injured hand."

Despite the physical limitations, I continued to work hard and find ways to adapt to the demands of the job, and I overcame the challenges and succeeded in my role.

In addition to the physical challenges, there were also moments of self-doubt and frustration. There were times when I questioned if I could keep up with the demands of the job. However, the support and encouragement from my colleagues and supervisors made a significant difference. They recognized my efforts and appreciated the hard work I put in every day.

As I reflect on these challenges, I realize that they taught me valuable lessons about perseverance. They reinforced the importance of a positive attitude and a strong work ethic. These qualities helped me succeed at Brown and enriched my personal life. Overcoming these obstacles gave me a sense of accomplishment and pride that I carry with me to this day.

Impact of Going Public

When Brown's stock went public, it brought about significant changes within the company. Managers who had been with the company for 20 years or more became instant millionaires. This shift in financial status created a new dynamic within the management team. The focus shifted from solely operational efficiency to also pleasing stockholders.

The pressure to meet stockholder expectations led to changes in various aspects of the company's operations. Decisions were no longer solely based on what was best for the company and its employees but also on what would satisfy the investors. This shift sometimes created tension and challenges as we adapted to the new priorities and expectations.

The impact of going public was felt across all levels of the organization. For many long-time employees, this transition was both exciting and challenging.

On one hand, there was a sense of pride in seeing the company reach new heights and gain recognition in the financial markets. On the other hand, the increased scrutiny and pressure to deliver results added a layer of complexity to our daily operations.

Managers had to balance the demands of the stockholders with the needs of the employees and the expectations of the customers. This balancing act was not always easy, and there were times when the priorities seemed to conflict. However, the core values of the company—integrity, service, and quality—remained our guiding principles.

In the midst of these changes, communication became more important than ever. Regular updates from the leadership team helped to keep everyone informed and aligned with the company's goals. Open forums and feedback sessions provided opportunities for employees to voice their concerns and suggestions. This transparent approach helped to build trust and grow a sense of unity during a time of significant transformation.

Changes in Daily Operations

One of the noticeable changes over time was in the cleanliness of our trucks. In the past, our trucks were washed every day, regardless of the weather conditions. Rain, sleet, or snow, a clean truck was a standard we upheld. However, as the years went by, this standard started to slip. Toward the end of my career, I often found myself frustrated with the state of my truck.

I would tell my manager, "I can't stand it no more. I'm going to wash my truck!" This change in daily operations reflected a broader shift in the company's priorities. Maintaining a clean and professional appearance was no longer as high on the agenda as it once was. Despite these changes, I remained committed to the standards I had always upheld.

Whenever someone from Atlanta, Brown's corporate office, would visit the center, I would make a point to speak up. I would tell them, "Go back and tell everyone it's not too late. We can make this company the 'tightest ship in the shipping business' once again. We can clean the trucks, clean up the driver group, and even go back to the old 'bow tie' law." This plea was my way of advocating for a return to the values and standards that had made Brown great.

The shift in daily operations extended beyond the cleanliness of our trucks. It also impacted how we approached customer service and operational efficiency. There was a growing emphasis on meeting deadlines and optimizing routes to ensure timely deliveries. While these goals were important, I often felt that the personal touch and attention to detail were being overlooked.

The decline in truck cleanliness was symptomatic of a larger issue. It represented a move away from the pride we once took in our work. Clean trucks were a symbol of our commitment to quality and professionalism. They were visible proof of our dedication to providing the best possible service to our customers.

Despite these changes, many of us continued to uphold the old standards. We took it upon ourselves to maintain the cleanliness of our trucks and to deliver exceptional service. We believed that these small acts of dedication would make a difference and help preserve the legacy of excellence that Brown was known for.

Appearance and Professional Standards

Throughout my career at Brown, maintaining a professional appearance was a core value. The founder of Brown, Jim Casey, emphasized the importance of clean, neat, and professional-looking drivers. He believed that the appearance of our drivers was a reflection of the company's values and commitment to excellence.

The reason for the brown uniform was simple—it didn't show dirt. This practical choice ensured that our drivers always looked presentable, even after a long day on the road. However, in recent years, I noticed a decline in the appearance standards of some of our drivers. This shift was concerning, as it went against the principles that Jim Casey had established.

Seeing drivers who did not uphold these standards was disappointing. Jim Casey loved his drivers and wanted them to take pride in their appearance. Maintaining these standards was about more than just looking good; it was about representing the company with professionalism and respect.

The decline in appearance standards was not just about uniforms. It extended to personal grooming and overall presentation. In the past, drivers were expected to be clean-shaven, with neatly trimmed hair and polished shoes. These details may seem minor, but they contributed to a professional image that instilled confidence in our customers.

Maintaining these standards requires discipline and commitment. It was not always easy to look polished after a long day of deliveries, but we understood the importance of these expectations. Customers trusted us with their packages, and our appearance played a role in building that trust.

In conversations with my colleagues, we often reminisced about the pride we took in our appearance. We shared stories of how customers would compliment us on our neat uniforms and professional demeanor. These interactions reinforced the value of maintaining high standards and reminded us of the legacy we were part of.

Improvements in Truck Design

One of the most significant improvements over the years has been in the design of our trucks. I spent twelve years driving a P500, followed by an International Diesel. These trucks required constant gear shifting and had no power steering, making them physically demanding to drive.

The steps of these older trucks were twice as high as the new ones, leading to frequent injuries. Missing the steps was common; sometimes, you could hear your driver scream. Every driver who operated these old trucks has scar tissue on their right leg from kneecap to ankle.

Fortunately, the introduction of modern, comfortable trucks has transformed our work environment. I finished my career in a GMC Workhorse automatic, V-8 fuel-injected, stepping out over the line. At times, I drove it like I stole it, but I was always on my side of the road. The newer trucks provided a level of comfort and safety that was unimaginable in the early days.

The new trucks were equipped with power steering, automatic transmissions, and ergonomic seats. These features significantly reduced the physical strain on drivers and improved overall safety. The improved design also included better suspension systems, which made for a smoother ride and less wear and tear on our bodies.

In addition to these practical improvements, the new trucks were designed with aesthetics in mind. Sleek, modern designs replaced the old, boxy look. The trucks were not only more functional but also more visually appealing. This attention to design reflected the company's commitment to maintaining a professional image.

Heat In The Brown Truck

In the South, where humidity is high, and temperatures often exceed 90 degrees, the heat inside a Brown truck can be unbearable. I used to call it the "Brown Microwave" because the truck is brown, the uniform is brown, and you sit on top of the engine, making the end of the day feel like being cooked. If Hell is hotter, believe me, you don't want to go.

The extreme heat was a serious concern, leading to instances of drivers passing out from heatstroke. I drank more water in July and August than I did all year in order to stay hydrated.

Sometimes, drivers had to be taken off their routes due to heat exhaustion. The company provided cold water at the terminal for everyone, which was a lifesaver during the hottest months.

The heat didn't bother me as much when I was younger, but as I got older, it became more difficult to handle.

Brown's Growth

Brown's growth over the years has been impressive. The company expanded its international presence, sponsoring the Olympics and having a car in NASCAR. These marketing initiatives raised the company's profile and showcased its capabilities on a global stage.

However, as the company grew, it became clear that maintaining its foundational values was crucial for long-term success. The focus on impeccable service, professional-looking drivers, and clean trucks was what made Brown a leader in the industry. These core principles should remain at the forefront of the company's operations.

The sponsorship of major events like the Olympics and NASCAR provided opportunities for brand visibility and recognition. It positioned Brown as a major player in the global market and reinforced its reputation for excellence. These initiatives were exciting and brought a sense of pride to the employees who saw their company represented on such prestigious platforms.

However, with this growth came new challenges. Expanding into international markets required dealing with different regulations, cultures, and customer expectations. It was a learning curve for the company, but it also provided opportunities for innovation and adaptation.

Call to Return to Basics

For Brown to remain relevant and successful in the future, it needs to return to the basics. This means emphasizing impeccable service, ensuring that drivers maintain a professional appearance, and keeping the trucks clean. These fundamental values were the cornerstone of Brown's success and should not be overlooked.

The belief in the importance of clean trucks as a form of advertising is something I have always advocated for. A clean truck not only looks good but also sends a message about the company's commitment to quality and professionalism. By returning to these basics, Brown can continue to build on its legacy and ensure its place as a leader in the shipping industry.

The return to basics involves more than just operational practices. It's about developing a culture of excellence and pride in our work. It means investing in our employees, providing them with the training and resources they need to succeed, and recognizing their contributions to the company's success.

By focusing on the core values that have defined Brown, the company can handle the challenges of the modern marketplace while staying true to its roots. It's about striking a balance between innovation and tradition, leveraging new technologies while maintaining the standards of service and professionalism that have set us apart.

As we look to the future, it's important to remember the lessons of the past. The principles that guided us in the early days are still relevant today. By adhering to these values, Brown can continue to thrive and maintain its reputation as the "tightest ship in the shipping business."

Every time I see a Brown truck, my mind is flooded with memories. I used to say the only things that will be left in the end are cockroaches and Brown trucks. This company has been a significant part of my life, and I am proud of the work we have done.

I would like to end this chapter with words from our founder, Jim Casey, that are etched on my retirement plaque: "Our horizon is as distant as our mind's eye wishes it to be." These words reflect the limitless potential of the company and the vision that has driven its success.

The journey with Brown has been long and rewarding. The experiences, challenges, and achievements have shaped who I am today. As I reflect on my career, I am filled with gratitude for the opportunities and the people who have been part of this journey. Brown is more than just a company; it's a community, a family with a commitment to excellence.

The memories and lessons from my time at Brown will stay with me forever. I hope that my observations and reflections in this chapter will inspire others to continue the legacy of excellence and uphold the values that have made Brown the remarkable company it is today.

CHAPTER 15
Retirement Day — The Cake with Your Name on It

I used to kid other drivers about how I was looking forward to the cake with my name on it. It was a long-standing tradition in our company that every retiree would be honored with a personalized cake. It was more than just a cake; it was a symbol of years of hard work, dedication, and the countless miles driven.

Besides the cake, retirees also received a beautifully etched piece of Crystal with words from our founder, Jim Casey. It served as a memento, a reminder of the values and principles upon which the company was built.

Additionally, each retiree got to pick a gift from a catalog, ranging from practical items to sentimental keepsakes. Retirement day was a significant milestone, and for me, it was filled with mixed emotions.

Anticipation and Circumstances

As my retirement day approached, I felt a mixture of excitement and apprehension. The anticipation was intense.

I had spent 34 years with the company, and the thought of walking away from a routine I had known for so long was both thrilling and daunting.

The night before my retirement, I received a call from my cousin. She informed me that she had just taken my mama to the hospital. My heart sank. I knew where I was headed after my speech the next day.

On the day of my retirement, I made the decision to deliver my speech outside. My thoughts were preoccupied with my mother's health, and I couldn't bring myself to walk into the building for the last time.

I informed the manager that the part-timers could eat my "cake," and they devoured it with enthusiasm. The cake, which I had looked forward to for years, was enjoyed by others, a small but significant gesture that marked the end of my career.

I must admit, I've never seen a tighter circle of Brownshirts. My colleagues gathered around, their expressions a mix of admiration and sadness.

Over the years, I witnessed many retirement speeches that expressed the bond shared among drivers. I had seen drivers cry, freeze, and struggle to find the words to express their emotions. On my retirement day, I also found myself in a similar position.

Retirement Day Speech

There was so much I wanted to say, but my mind was with my mother. My speech was simple but heartfelt. I reminded my colleagues to remember that if they were having a bad day, it wasn't the customer's fault. "The customer is not always right," I said, "but they are still the customer."

As I stood there, delivering my speech, I reflected on my 34 years with the company. I felt fortunate to have had a secure job for so long, especially in an industry that could be unpredictable. I was proud to be a Teamster for 34 years. Being part of a union provided a sense of camaraderie and support that was invaluable.

In my speech, I emphasized the importance of using the horn and waving—a small act of acknowledgment that could make a big difference in a driver's day.

After I finished my speech, our principal officer of Local Union 61 stepped into the circle. He spoke about my dedication and reliability, highlighting that I had been a Teamster from the beginning to the end. His words made me feel proud of how I had conducted myself over the years.

The Perks of My Retirement

One of the most significant aspects of my retirement was the opportunity to spend time with my mother in her last days. I felt incredibly lucky to be retired and to have the chance to be there for her. I kept her room filled with flowers, transforming it into a floral shop because she loved flowers so much. This small act of kindness brought her joy and comfort, and it was a way for me to show my love and appreciation.

Encounters with Retired Drivers

During my career, I often met retired drivers along my route. One day, I encountered two retired drivers at a farm supply store. We struck up a conversation, and I asked them how retirement was going.

Their response was candid: "All we do now is go to the doctor." At the time, I didn't fully understand what they meant. It wasn't until I retired that I began to comprehend the toll a long career could take on one's body.

After going "balls to the wall" for 34 years, I realized that my body was damaged goods. The years of hard work and physical exertion had left their mark.

Post-Retirement Realization About My Health

As Thanksgiving approached, I set a personal goal: to make it through the year without ending up in the hospital. It would be the first time since I retired that I hadn't been hospitalized. This goal was a reflection of my determination to stay healthy and make the most of my retirement. My time as a soldier had prepared me for this new phase of life. The discipline I learned in the military was invaluable as I faced the challenges of retirement.

In the Army, there was a saying that I often shared with my troops: "Take the pain. Pain lets you know you are still alive. Turn it into something positive!" This mantra became even more relevant in retirement. Despite the physical discomfort and health issues, I reminded myself to stay positive and make the best of each day. Delicately, I aimed to get out unscathed.

Reflecting on my fellow retirees, I realized that many of them faced similar challenges. Of all the drivers I had retired with, four had passed away. The others, with very few exceptions, spent much of their time visiting doctors.

Post-Retirement Social Interactions

Despite the challenges, I miss my customers. During my career, I interacted with around 200 people a day. Now, in retirement, I might talk to three people in a day. This drastic reduction in social interaction was an adjustment, and it made me nostalgic for the bustling days of my career.

My life now is a reminder of the Statler Brothers' song "Flowers on the Wall." The lyrics resonate with my experience of retirement.

I often run into customers at Wally World, and some recognize me despite the changes in my appearance. One customer, noticing me staring at him, asked, "Is that you?" His question reminded me of Robin Williams in "Peter Pan," a character who had to rediscover his true self. Like Peter Pan, I was adapting to a new phase of life, trying to keep moving with a positive attitude.

Future Outlook

In my retirement days, I find myself hoping and praying for my country. I want to leave it better for my grandchildren and for everyone's grandchildren. This desire is a driving force in my life, a way to stay connected to a sense of purpose. As my grandmother promised, I aim to leave behind a rose garden—a symbol of beauty and hope for future generations.

Retirement day was a milestone filled with mixed emotions. It marked the end of a long and fulfilling career and the beginning of a new chapter.

As I go through this new phase of my life, I reflect on the lessons I learned, the friendships I made, and the legacy I hope to leave behind.

Retirement is not just an end; it is an opportunity to cherish the past and embrace the future. Through it all, the cake with my name on it remains a symbol of the journey, the years of hard work, and the community that supported me along the way.

CHAPTER 16
Conclusion—Why I Wrote This Book

Folks, here we go. The reality of our roads today is that traffic will only increase over time. Our cities are expanding, more people are getting behind the wheel, and the roads are becoming busier than ever. This is why I felt compelled to write this book. I challenge anyone who reads this to become a more "Courteous Driver." It's a simple yet powerful concept. Courtesy on the road is contagious, and it can significantly reduce the stress and danger associated with driving.

When we think about driving, we often focus on the mechanics of operating a vehicle—accelerating, braking, steering. But there's so much more to it than that. Driving is a complex activity that requires not only physical skills but also a great deal of mental and emotional awareness. It's about being aware of your surroundings, anticipating the actions of other drivers, and making quick decisions. And most importantly, it's about being courteous and respectful to everyone on the road.

Witnessing and Experiencing Crashes

Over the years, I have witnessed and been involved in several crashes. These experiences have taught me invaluable lessons about the importance of being a courteous and careful driver.

When a crash happens, it happens so quickly that it can make your head spin. One moment, you are driving along, and the next, you are dealing with the aftermath of a collision. It is a jarring experience that can have lasting effects on your confidence and peace of mind.

One of the most critical lessons I have learned is the importance of slowing down. Speed is often a significant factor in crashes. The faster you are going, the less time you have to react to unexpected situations.

By simply reducing your speed, you can give yourself more time to respond and potentially avoid a collision. This is particularly important in areas with heavy traffic or poor visibility.

Another crucial lesson is to avoid distracted driving. In our fast-paced world, it's easy to become distracted while driving. Whether it's checking your phone, adjusting the radio, or even having an intense conversation with a passenger, distractions can take your attention away from the road. The conversation can wait. Your primary focus should always be on driving. When you are behind the wheel, everything else should take a backseat.

Importance of Space and Visibility

It all boils down to space and visibility. These are two of the most critical factors in driving safely. Maintaining adequate space between your vehicle and others gives you the necessary buffer to react to sudden changes.

Whether it is a car suddenly braking in front of you or an unexpected obstacle appearing in your path, having enough space allows you to maneuver safely.

Visibility is equally important. Always ensure that your windows and mirrors are clean and properly adjusted. This might seem like a small detail, but it can make a significant difference in your ability to see and react to your surroundings. Good visibility helps you anticipate potential hazards and drive safely.

Teaching My Granddaughter to Drive

I had the pleasure of teaching my granddaughter to drive. It was an experience that reminded me of the importance of patience and clear communication. I know she got tired of me constantly reminding her about the fundamentals of driving, but those reminders paid off.

Two years later, she has no tickets and no accidents. She has been rewarded with her dream car, a Jeep, and is now a freshman at East Carolina University.

Teaching someone to drive is about more than just showing them how to operate a vehicle. It's about instilling good habits and reinforcing the importance of safety.

I made sure to emphasize the importance of being a courteous driver, maintaining space and visibility, and avoiding distractions. These are lessons that will serve her well throughout her driving career.

Final Driving Tips

As a final tip, I will share something I told the Driver Group on my retirement day. Don't be afraid to use your horn. It's a tool for communication, and it can help prevent accidents. A quick honk can alert other drivers to your presence or warn them of potential hazards. It has kept me from harm too many times to mention.

Another piece of advice I used to give to drivers in the morning is to keep it between the ditches and always shiny side up. This simple phrase encapsulates the essence of safe driving. Stay on the road, avoid obstacles, and keep your vehicle in good condition. It's a straightforward yet powerful reminder to drive carefully and responsibly.

Addressing Road Rage

One of the most concerning issues on the road today is road rage. It is a dangerous and escalating problem that can lead to serious accidents and even violence.

Road rage has got to stop. If you find yourself in a situation where another driver is displaying aggressive behavior, the best course of action is to de-escalate. Slow down, get away from the aggressive driver, and do not engage. Nothing is worth causing an accident or worse.

Road rage often stems from frustration and impatience. By practicing patience and courtesy, you can help reduce the likelihood of road rage incidents. Remember, everyone on the road is dealing with their own challenges and stresses. A little patience and understanding can go a long way in creating a safer and more pleasant driving environment for everyone.

As I reflect on the journey that led me to write this book, I am reminded of the importance of trust and compassion. I yearn for the day we all, as Americans, treat each other as we did after 9/11, and we can create a better driving environment and a better society. Patience in everything we do and compassion for each other will only lead to a greater America.

Driving is more than just a means of getting from one place to another. It's an opportunity to practice patience, courtesy, and compassion. These practices will surely lead to a greater America!

By becoming a more courteous driver, you can make the roads safer and more pleasant for everyone.

Thank you for reading this book, and I hope that the lessons shared here will inspire you to drive with greater awareness and kindness.